Migrating toward Happiness

The Soundtrack to My Spiritual Awakening

Tara O'Grady

BALBOA.
PRESS

A DIVISION OF HAY HOUSE

Balboa Press books may be ordered through booksellers or by contacting:

Balboa Press
A Division of Hay House
1663 Liberty Drive
Bloomington, IN 47403
www.balboapress.com
1 (877) 407-4847

Print information available on the last page.

ISBN: 978-1-9822-2100-3 (sc)
ISBN: 978-1-9822-2099-0 (hc)
ISBN: 978-1-9822-2104-1 (e)

Library of Congress Control Number: 2019901060

Balboa Press rev. date: 02/08/2019

Dedicated to my grandparents: Nora Conaghan, Pat Conaghan, Catherine O'Grady, and Padraic O'Grady

All the grandmothers and grandfathers have stories and if you let them die without taking down their stories you are criminal.

—Frank McCourt, *Teacher Man*

Author's Note

The events in this book of nonfiction are all true, including the dreams and supernatural occurrences. The people I encountered along the journey are real souls; however, I changed some of their names and addresses to protect their privacy. My family told me their stories as they remembered them, and they shared many photographs from their past, which inspired me to embark on my adventures. I write in my journal daily, so the dreams, conversations, and songs are always fresh in my mind. I even researched my diaries from as far back as the age of eight to discover things I had forgotten. My soul's purpose is to help you remember what you have forgotten. When I was initially writing the book, I knew the stories were extraordinary and meant to inspire, but I didn't fully realize during the events as they unfolded that I was experiencing an awakening to the magic and mysteries of the Universe. Sometimes it takes a lifetime to wake up. Looking back, I now understand that I've been guided to share what I have learned. And what's that, you ask? Nat King Cole spells it out for you: L-O-V-E.

Contents

Prologue

As if in an intoxicated state, I trip over a garden hose as my eyes chase the winged beauties upon entering the butterfly conservatory at the Bronx Zoo. They flitter and fly and zigzag, dazzling my eyes with their glorious colors. I leap into their delicate dance like a giddy schoolgirl, hoping to catch the kiss of a speckled wing across my cheek. Dozens of butterflies flutter above and around me. Classical music creates an inspiring backdrop to their fickle performance. I close my eyes to steady my stance but can't contain the pure elation building within my chest. Dizzy with pleasure, seduced by their flight, I lift a finger, hoping one of these exquisite creatures will be tempted to use it as a perch. Not one accepts my flirtatious advances. Leaning over their nectar bar, I inhale the fragrant lilacs and wildflowers on which they choose to land. Sighing blissfully, I am in awe of these miraculous reincarnated spirits. The monarchs charm the skin off me. How lovely to be enchanted on an ordinary Tuesday.

With Mozart playing on a hidden speaker, the greenhouse is transformed into a dance hall, and I am seventeen again, waltzing with my Austrian friend's brother at my first ball in Vienna and laughing hysterically as my strapless sequined gown inches its way down my chest like a caterpillar shedding its skin. The greenhouse feels like a summer firefly jar containing every kiss I've ever tasted, captured, and released at the same luminous moment, electrifying my senses in a rapturous, melodious, heavenly delirium.

This must be what heaven feels like. Maybe this is the feeling Alberto described when he floated above his body after the accident.

I had forgotten that feeling, the feeling of not wearing a watch or knowing what day it is, of sitting close to the curb and fingering the pebbles, of sucking on ice pops and orange wedges, of being barefoot and talking to my toes. *Hello, toes.*

A young day camp leader enters the greenhouse with a small group of children. They immediately begin pointing, shouting, and leaping, trying to capture the butterflies as their leader scolds them. It is impossible for her to get their attention. But then the zoologist enters the space.

"Is this Sunshine Day Camp?" she asks in a pleasant tone.

"Yes!" the children respond in unison.

"My name is Tabitha, and I work here at the Bronx Zoo. Your counselor informed me that you are learning about butterflies. Is that correct?"

"Yes!" They don't look at Tabitha because their eyes can't help but follow the insects zigging this way and zagging that way.

"Okay, great. Well then, what can you tell me about butterflies?" she cleverly asks rather than lecturing them on the stages of metamorphosis.

"These orange ones are called monarchs," one girl says.

"Very good, and what do you know about the monarch butterfly?"

A boy jumps up and down, waving his hand, and shouts his answer before the zoologist spots him. "Ooh, miss! They fly south for winter just like birds."

"Yes, that's right. The monarch butterfly is the only butterfly that migrates both south and north, making the long journey from Canada to Mexico. But can one butterfly make the round-trip?"

Many children shout, "No!" and then another boy speaks above the rest.

"Only one generation can take the journey because they fly like three thousand miles, which is, like, really, really far. Then their offspring fly back in spring."

"Very good. Wow, you guys really know your stuff. How do the monarchs know where to go?"

"They use OnStar. My dad has that in his car," a girl jokes, and the group breaks into hysterics.

"Actually, you aren't too far off," Tabitha responds with a smile. "The monarchs can use the earth's magnetic field for orientation, using their antennae as a compass—or navigational system, as you put it—but they also have inherited the flight patterns. It's instinctual and passed down through generations. They just know where to go."

One girl who has been quietly observing and listening slowly raises her hand until her counselor notices her in the corner of the greenhouse.

"Felicidad, do you have a question?" the camp leader asks the shy girl, and she shakes her head. "Then do you have a comment?"

The girl nods and speaks in a quiet voice so that everyone has to stop moving in order to hear her. Even the butterflies seem to temporarily cease their fluttering.

"My grandmother celebrates Dia de los Muertos when the butterflies arrive in Mexico," Felicidad whispers.

"Can you tell us what that is?" Tabitha asks.

"It's the day after Halloween, November first. *Mi abuela* believes the butterflies are the souls of our ancestors coming back home."

Even the butterflies consider the November moon significant, I think to myself.

Part 1: Chrysalis

1

(In My) Solitude—Billie Holiday

I step into the subway car at the elevated Sixty-First Street Woodside Station after standing in the assaulting drizzle of an early morning shower and squeeze my way into a pocket of space to find myself pressed up against a man who's wearing a damp suit and listening to his iPod.

My parents met at a dance. My grandparents met at a dance. The closest I get to being pressed up against a man while music is playing is during rush hour.

I brace myself as the train lurches out of the station. I brace myself for the eight-hour shift that lies before me—eight hours of mindless tedium behind a desk, eight hours to wallow in how utterly single I am, eight hours to daydream about the other life I should be living, the one with romance and travel. The one where I don't sit behind that damned desk.

I eventually get a seat when the crowds push their way off at Queensboro Plaza, sandwiched between an Asian woman reading a newspaper in her native tongue and a Latino whose head keeps bobbing as the conductor mumbles the name of each station.

I open my weekly news magazine and return to an article about Alice Ramsey, the first woman to cross the American landscape by car in 1909. She and her three female passengers took fifty-nine days to drive from Manhattan to San Francisco. Those were daring women ahead of their time. I often daydream about taking a similar journey. I wonder what the roads were like back then. According to the article, the golden age of the road trip was in the fifties, when highways opened up and America experienced a boom in car manufacturing after the war. There is a sidenote with a quote from John Steinbeck: "Every American hungers to move."

We are descended from those who moved, immigrants searching for a better life. The problem is, most of us can't just pack up and leave. We have responsibilities. We have day jobs. We have headaches.

My head is too foggy from my early morning rise to fully escape into the magazine, so I stare at the floor. My thoughts have no particular focus until a young couple boards the train at Hunters Point Avenue. They stand together quietly with their elegant arms extending up to the bars overhead. They wear trench coats in conservative navy and beige hues. They balance themselves, holding their coffees and umbrellas. It is obvious they have been together for many moons. They don't wear wedding rings. This is their morning ritual. They are bright and fresh and eager to begin the day together. No words ever pass between them, but they communicate in the most intimate way I have ever seen in public.

Right in front of everyone on the train, although I'm the only one watching, the woman crosses her leg and places her foot alongside the man's foot, and then he returns the gesture so that his foot is aligned with hers. They look at their feet, a left foot and a right foot, pressed up against each other. They smile in unison and lift their heads slowly until they meet each other's gaze. They linger for a moment in each other's eyes and then look away. I feel like a privileged stalker to have witnessed such a simple expression of love. But my heart sinks. Where is my Monday morning escort to work? My lover man with his coffee and trench coat? My right shoe?

When the train crawls into Grand Central Station, the doors open, and the couple disappears into a sea of heads. I watch their feet walk away together before the doors close, and then I sigh and shut my eyes until the train enters Times Square. The sleepy Latino who's been using my shoulder as a pillow awakens with a jerk and stumbles toward the door. The Asian woman pushes her way ahead of me, and I sulk through the Forty-Second Street station.

As I ascend the escalator, I hear music. The usual African drums and sounds of other street musicians aren't filling the tunnels. Today a violin sings through the station. I recognize the melody but can't recall where I know it from. I rise higher and higher from the depths of the underground. A smile grows on my face. I begin to hum along with the tune as the lyrics reveal themselves to me about climbing mountains, fording streams, and following rainbows until you find your dream.

Julie Andrews. "The Sound of Music."

"Thank you, Granny," I say to myself. "Yes, I'll keep that in mind."

I enter my building and flash my ID at the guard, but he's having a staring contest with his shoes. I make my way to the elevator, where a cluster of people gather silently, waiting for it to arrive. They also have a keen interest in their feet. When the doors open, the employees file one by one into the space, choose a corner or pocket, and adjust their stance in order to maintain a comfortable distance. Once the doors close and the button for each floor has been designated, we stand, we stare, we rise. In silence.

When the elevator reaches my floor, I walk to my cubicle and see that the coworker who sits across from me is engrossed in online news at his computer. I notice he is wearing his cardigan inside out.

"Morning," I mumble, but he doesn't respond. *Seriously, it can't be that engrossing*, I think to myself.

I automatically turn on my computer and take off my raincoat. The dust I've disturbed on the deserted desk next to mine alerts my allergies, and I sneeze loudly. I wait in expectation for a cordial response. Nothing.

"Bless you," I whisper to the space between us with a pinch of irritation.

My workday begins.

The phone is ringing on my desk at my not-for-profit organization. I glance up from the colorful map of America, the one on the back page of the *New York Times* with the weather report. I've drawn a line from New York to Seattle using my number-two pencil. I've been staring at the map for hours, days, and weeks, calculating miles, gas prices, and hotel fees. On my lunch hour, I research tourist sites along the route, such as Mount Rushmore and Yellowstone National Park, and list entrance fees.

I've written out two scenarios in columns on a yellow pad: "If I Don't Get Laid Off" and "If I Do Get Laid Off."

"If I Don't Get Laid Off" means I'll have two weeks' vacation to drive across America this summer. It means I won't have much time to even stop at Mount Rushmore—or stop at all, for that matter. Perhaps I will rent a car, leave it in Seattle, and then fly back. But that is pricy.

"If I Do Get Laid Off" means I'll have plenty of time to stop awhile in Yellowstone, but the longer I am on the road, the more hotel fees will add up, and I still have to drive my Toyota back east, which means gas calculations will double.

This is how I have been spending my time in my office, where my supervisor yells at me daily for sending emails she hasn't proofread, as she likes to micromanage the trajectory of ants making a hill.

There are other lists and images posted on the walls of my cubicle that distract me from my work, which I don't have much of these days due to the budgets being diminished. Below numerous postcards featuring images of Audrey Hepburn, my idol, whom I worship when I stand before my closet, wondering what she would wear to work, next to the landscapes of Ireland I have cut out from years of old calendars so that when I look up from my computer, I see green fields, stone walls, cottages, and the sea, there is a list entitled "Things I've Always Wanted to Do."

Things I've Always Wanted to Do
Swim naked

Learn to play ukulele
Drive exceptionally fast
Ride in hot air balloon with Sean Connery
Wear a dress designed for me
Take a cooking class
Hang out with Bono in a Dublin pub
Drink tea with geisha in Japan
Tour all of Canada with Michael Bublé in a hot tub
Attend an Oscar ceremony
Learn to read music
Speak Spanish fluently
Swing dance at Graceland in the jungle room
Fly around Hogwarts on my broom
Find love

I also have a number of Post-it notes with names of the many places I want to visit, including but not limited to Saint Lucia, Barcelona, any chocolate shop in Belgium, Istanbul, and Tierra del Fuego, the southernmost tip of South America.

My phone is still ringing. I don't recognize the number, but the caller ID shows the name B. Grant, and I know there is a Barbara up in HR. This could be it.

"This is Tara."

"Tara, Barbara Grant. Can you please come up to the eleventh floor?"

I feel the first drop of rain on my face. The anticipated storm has arrived, and I smile as I gently place the receiver back in its cradle.

Barbara directs me into her supervisor's office, where I am met by the head of human resources and the executive director of my department, both of whom are wearing grave expressions.

"I think you know why you are here," the head of HR says as I take a seat and smile at her, half listening, wondering what I am going to pack, whom I will take on the journey, and when I can escape and begin my new life.

I know why I am sitting here. The sky is falling. The budgets were cut, and employees are expendable, just like coffee and staplers. I've been waiting for this moment. I've wanted it. I have spent enough time sitting at my desk, waiting for my life to begin beyond a cubicle. It is time to move. It is time for change.

I noticed last year how we cut back on little things, such as paper and pencil sharpeners, but then the complimentary Starbucks coffee was cut, and chocolate chip cookies suddenly stopped appearing on the table at meetings. That was devastating. Some staff were let go last summer, hence the dusty, deserted desks. That's when I began my backup plan, though outlining America with a number-two pencil didn't occur until about mid-January, when I usually begin to plan my annual trips and vacations for the upcoming year.

"Do you have any questions?" My director is looking at me as I look out the window and see that the sky is clearing.

"When do I begin—I mean leave?" I can't contain my elation.

"Two weeks. You seem to be taking the news rather well." The head of HR is trying to read my face.

"Oh." I smile at her. "Well, I have a lot of things I've always wanted to do."

This is a gift, I say to myself as I skip past Barbara, who peeks up at me from her desk. I am not the first person she has called up to the eleventh floor today. I don't envy her—or the colleagues I find crying at their desks as I return to mine to look again at my Audrey Hepburn postcards, images of Ireland, and map of America sprawled across my desk. I probably would have stayed in this position because it is a job in a field I am passionate about, but I have become stale in this space, wilting like an outdoor plant mistakenly placed indoors and nowhere near a sunbathed window. I am not growing. If they hadn't pushed me off this airplane, I probably wouldn't have jumped, because part of me really likes security. However, if we never take chances, we never get to answer the what-ifs of our lives.

2

New York State of Mind—Billy Joel

My apartment in New York is sandwiched between multitudes of commuter pathways. On one side is the lovely Queens Boulevard, nicknamed the Boulevard of Death due to the high number of pedestrians hit by cars each year. On the other side, the Long Island Railroad rumbles under a tunnel that shakes the foundation of my home. Overhead is the direct path of jets landing at LaGuardia airport every three to five minutes. Then there is the Number Seven subway line, elevated above my street, nicknamed the International Express. It streams its way across the tracks like a needle through Queens neighborhoods, stitching them together like a quilt, with a patch of Colombia here, a pattern of Greece there, and a bit of green in the middle, representing my Irish-Korean neighborhood. I have a few trees on my street—just enough green to remind me that nature does indeed exist.

New York is cluttered with concrete and steel. There are a number of parks, but no matter how deep you escape into a park, a horn or menacing siren will always find you. The billboards, cell phones, and traffic, both vehicular and pedestrian, are all distractions. The landscape of New York City is one that I have grown accustomed to. I was born here. I can function in this space. I know its rhythms. I move with it as one moves with a herd of buffalo so as not to get trampled. But these pathways, highways, subways, and motorways are all taking me away from a natural landscape, one that allows me to imagine, reflect, dream, and feed my spirit.

I tend to feel connected to my spirit only when I am in Ireland, where my mother and grandparents were born. There is something mystical about that land. The ghosts of my ancestors walk through those peaceful valleys speckled with purple heather and cluttered only with cattle or sheep causing the occasional road block for the unfortunate tourist. The rhythm of the ocean lapping the Donegal shoreline has the ability to change one's breathing pattern. My breathing in New York City is shallow. I'd rather not deeply inhale exhaust from taxis and delivery trucks.

My name is Tara O'Grady. When I say it out loud in New York City, it is natural to hear one of two responses: "Nice Jewish name!" or "So you're Italian then?" This is indeed a melting pot with a sense of humor, and I am just another ingredient.

My mother has brought me to her homeland every summer since I was an infant. That's where I experienced my first road trip.

"She gets car sick," she explained to my uncle, who kicked a stone into an empty field as he lit his third cigarette with his back to the wind. The journey from Dublin made me lose my morning feed of tea and toast as my uncle tore up the road to Donegal. The roads had a bit of a bend in them back then, before wider and more direct motorways were developed. They wrapped around farms, outlining the patches of a green quilt stitched together by hedges, stone walls, and barbed wire. I couldn't see out the side windows, as I was sandwiched between suitcases and duffel bags, gasping for fresh air as my brother licked his greasy fingers while alternating between salt-and-vinegar chips and Mars bars.

"You're all right, love." My mother rubbed my back as she looked out into damp fields. I couldn't tell if tears or rain fell onto her cheeks.

She too suffered from motion sickness. The boat that took her to America under the November moon made certain she would regret her journey. But since then, she has flown across the Atlantic annually, and together we returned to her mother's arms, arms that crushed me with love.

I knew the country roads like the lines on Granny's face. Even with my eyes closed, I could tell where we were. We now enter Donegal through the Pettigo road, recognized by its bumps and potholes that awaken me from my jet-lagged slumber. But back then, my uncle usually avoided crossing the borders into Northern Ireland, where duffel bags were searched and passports inspected as I stared down the barrel of a soldier's gun. That was in the 1970s, when I noticed bumper stickers on American cars that read, "Free Bobby Sands." I didn't know who the young man was or why he was in a prison near Belfast, but I knew it mattered to the Irish in New York, to Catholics like us.

After we reached the Pettigo road, passed through Donegal Town, and stopped in Mountcharles for more cigarettes, a newspaper, or vanilla ice cream if my tummy could handle it by then, I knew to make a left off the main road where a bathtub filled with rainwater for cattle sat at the edge of a field. I knew to stop at the crossroads where my brother, Tommy, and I walked to buy sweets at Cassidy's. I knew to hold my breath and pray as my uncle sped up at the blind spot at the top of the narrow lane, where if one were to meet a tractor, the tractor would not end up in the ditch. I knew to make a final left down the gravel-covered road that led to my grandparents' farm, which my mother left in the autumn of 1957, when both tears and rain flooded her cheeks.

I would fall out of the car and into Granny's arms, and she'd carry me like the wind into her kitchen; fill my empty belly with her freshly baked bread; and place newborn kittens collected from neighboring farms, temporarily saved from their impending drowning, in my lap for my entertainment and delight. My grandfather, a silent mountain with loving blue eyes and massive hands used for picking potatoes, would tousle my hair until bits of earth fell from under his fingernails and across my eyelashes.

I knew they loved me with every pint of their blood. I could taste it in the milk Granny squeezed from her cows. I could smell it in the smoke Granddad teased from the turf fire. I could hear it in their prayers as they knelt at their bedside after they'd removed their teeth.

I treasured them in those summers as one admires the autumn leaves of red and gold. I knew I wouldn't have them forever.

3

American Pie—Don McLean

"Is this you?" I ask my father as I scan faded photographs in a shoebox he stores in the closet where he keeps his winter coats.

"Yes, this is your grandmother with me, Cack, and Peg in the Bronx." He points at a photo of his mother and sisters standing in front of a black car parked outside a tall brick apartment building on 176th Street. "And that's our 1940 Chevy."

"What were you—like three years old?" I ask, admiring his little sailor suit and white shoes.

"Um, yeah, that's 1944. Oh, and look at this one!" He finds another photograph and laughs at himself. "That's me, Peg, and a neighbor kid. Jerry was his name." He turns it over and reads the date. "October 1950. We loved westerns. Look at our cowboy hats and guns!" He smiles as if he's found a treasure chest.

"And this is when I was dating your mom. That's my 1964 Chevy in the garage in Little Neck." He lingers on the image, admiring my mother's turquoise paisley dress and Elizabeth Taylor hairstyle.

"Oh, look at this!" He pulls out a sepia-colored image on a photograph two inches by three inches. "That's my mother sitting on your grandfather's 1934 Chevy. Look at that car!"

"You only owned Chevys?" I notice most of the photographs have cars in the background.

"Are you kidding me? We were a Chevy family." He beams. "Look." He takes out another photograph. "This is Father Peter with his Chevy when we visited him out west." He shows me an image of his Irish uncle, who could have been his father with the resemblance. The handsome young priest from Roscommon wears a cowboy hat that hides his thick black curls, along with his black suit and priestly white collar. My father wears a white T-shirt, khaki pants, and Converse sneakers.

"I see wing tips in the background!" I say as I examine the photo more closely.

"Yep, that's the '57 Bel Air we drove out to visit Father Peter in Spokane," Dad says as he searches for a better image. "Look. This is us in the driveway in Little Neck when my parents brought home the new car."

He hands me the square image. The color in the photograph has faded. The Bel Air looks pink or mauve—I can't tell. My grandparents, my father, and one of my aunts are all sitting inside with their heads and elbows hanging out over the open windows.

My heart always skips a beat when I see that particular vehicle on the road—a rare sight. I get the same feeling as if I am seeing my first love go by.

"So why do I own a Toyota?" I look at my father, wondering why I never knew about this family legacy and devotion to an American manufacturer.

"Japanese cars got better over the years, and we started buying imports." He shrugs. "But back in the day, you were either a Chevy family or a Ford family. It was like picking a baseball team. And we hated Ford families. If you were born into a Chevy family, you were always a Chevy family."

"Is that why your Hyundai is parked in the driveway?"

He ignores my sarcasm. "Your grandfather loved Chevys when he came to this country. See this picture?" He picks up the image of his mother sitting on the 1934 Chevrolet. "Your Waterford grandmother was very impressed by this vehicle. Not many Irish men owned a car at that time. Your grandfather bought it in the heart of the Depression. This was one of their first dates. It was taken in 1937. They met at a dance, and he took her out for a ride in that car, and she married him within six months. She almost didn't marry him, though. Had cold feet on the steps of the church. It all happened too fast. But her girlfriends convinced her to marry him. They figured a fellow who had a car had money and stability. He was a catch."

"So she married him for his car?"

"Pretty much." He chuckles. "They weren't a match made in heaven. She was so full of life. She loved parties and music and having people around. She's the one who wanted to drive all the way out west to visit his brother, Father Peter. My father didn't want to go—couldn't be bothered. He assumed she'd turn around at the George Washington Bridge and come home. But she had wanderlust in her. She loved to just get in the car and go. One day she said, 'Let's go to Florida,' and within two hours, we were all packed and driving down south. That's what she was like."

He stares at his mother's image, and his thoughts take him far away, beyond the borders of the Bronx, over the bridges of his adult life, and through the tunnels to his childhood, where he keeps his memories underground.

I pull a picture from the shoebox. Its color has faded, but I can see her red hair. She is leaning against a concrete wall with red rocks and a waterfall behind her, wearing a white cap and a white sundress with blue and pink tulips. On the back of the photograph, one of her children has written, "Mom standing on Buffalo Bill Dam along Cody Road to Yellowstone, Wyoming." She is facing the photographer but not looking at the camera. Her gaze is up, looking out beyond the frame of the photograph. She can't be contained within the small frame. She looks as if she is ready to take flight.

"I just got laid off," I say as I keep my eyes on the photograph.

"You knew it was coming." My father shifts in his chair as my mother suddenly enters the kitchen. I didn't realize she was in earshot.

"What are you going to do now?" Her tone is full of worry. She left Ireland for the almighty dollar. It means everything to her.

"Well, I can finally take that road trip." I look at my dad, and he laughs.

"Tara, you need money, not a vacation." Mom is always the practical one. She once bought me a plaque from Shannon Airport that read, "Chocolate, Coffee, Men—Some Things Are Just Better Rich." She too believes in security.

"I have plenty of time to find another job. Besides, there aren't really any jobs out there to be found at the moment." I'm still holding the photograph of my father's mother in my hand.

"Well, how the hell are you going to pay for a bloody road trip?" Her Irish temper is flaring up, as is her financial fear of not having a pot to piss in.

"I haven't figured that out yet," I reply quietly, not wanting my dreams to be dashed before I have developed some sort of plan. I've always had a bit of a rebel spirit in me that reveals itself when necessary. If someone says I can't do something, I go out of my way to make it happen. I don't know where that comes from since my mother has always been so cautious and protective with me. Not wanting me to make waves, she kept me in a respectful shell my entire childhood, causing me to blush at the sharp tone of authority.

I look again at the redhead in a photograph that can't contain the woman within its frame. I decide I have to learn more about this woman since she died before my parents met. After all, she was my granny.

4

Nora—Traditional Irish Folk

I only had one granny growing up: Nora, my mother's mother. She was a hardworking Irish woman who rose with the sun, greeted God, milked her cows and put them out to field, cooked for her family, and threw her heart into life on the farm in Donegal, where my mother was born and where I spent every summer of my life far away from the concrete canyons and the hustle and bustle of the New York minute.

She's the one I speak to when I pray.

One day last winter, I was standing next to my small Toyota Matrix, trembling—not from the cold but from the idea of not being able to drive in a snowstorm.

Ever since I learned how to drive, I have been panicked about snowfall. Even a news report about the slight chance of flurries frightens me. There are hundreds of miles of streets that need to be cleared by sanitation workers in New York. Only main boulevards get plowed in Queens. The side streets become treacherous. Cars are abandoned by their owners in midtravel. Plows block parked cars with mountainous walls of blackened snow for weeks. I've driven in snow. It scares the hell out of me. There's nothing worse than feeling you have no control over your vehicle.

As I was slipping and sliding around my car and clearing the snow from each window, grumbling to myself about the weather, I thought about my granny Nora. She rarely complained about anything. She didn't have time to complain. There was too much to do. She rode her bicycle seven miles into town, as she didn't own a car or even know how to drive one, and I don't think she had to worry much about snow in Ireland—a frost maybe but rarely mountains of snow.

I, on the other hand, was worrying—so much that I began to pray. I needed a guardian angel to protect me. That's when a rooster walked by my car.

A rooster.

In a parking lot.

In New York City.

During a snowstorm.

The abnormal thing about my praying is not the act of doing it but, rather, whom I pray to. Lately I haven't been praying to God or any of the saints I was obsessed with as a child growing up in the Catholic educational system. I used to read biographies of the saints' lives the way kids today read celebrity gossip on their Twitter accounts. Lately I've been praying to my granny Nora, who passed away a few years ago. She wasn't a saint or anything. I just find great comfort in talking to her. I always did, especially when she was alive.

"Hi, Granny," I said to the rooster in the parking lot in New York City during a snowstorm.

We locked eyes for a moment, and I smiled at its cockiness. I suddenly felt calm and protected by the extraordinary creature that miraculously had appeared out of nowhere wearing its reddish-brown feathers with a hint of green shimmering upon its breast. Then I watched the bird strut away in all its magnificent plumage, with the long black tail feathers setting a dramatic contrast against the white snow.

After I scraped the ice from my windshield, I carefully drove through the blinding whiteout with confidence and arrived safely at my destination.

5

Lookin' for Love (In All the Wrong Places)—Johnny Lee

I'm feeling confident today as I climb up the elevated subway station in Queens. I have a few weeks to figure out how to make this road trip work financially. Well, technically, I have ages since I have no other job offers at the moment. I walk along the crowded, sunbathed platform and see a strapping lad standing alone with a cup of coffee in one hand and the nook of his pocket in the other. He has white paint speckled on his work boots, and despite his muscular, intimidating frame, he slouches slightly with the melancholy of an immigrant.

I have succumbed to stalking men on the subway. I realized I was spending quite a lot of time going back and forth between work and home—thirty minutes each way, one hour each day, five hours per week. Why not make use of that time? Some people read on their commute; others sleep. I stalk.

Sometimes I stand on the platform of a busy station, spot a fellow, size him up visually, and then follow him onto whichever train he gets on next.

Today I feel brave as the train arrives, and I rush with the crowd to follow him inside. I let the other passengers push their way to the available seats. I assume he will stand, and I want to stand near him so I can strike up a conversation.

My back is against the doors, and his back is facing me. I am inches from his pale, freckled neck. His short haircut exposes skin untouched by the sun above his denim shirt collar.

"You left Ireland for this?" I say loudly enough for him to hear me over the hum of the train on the tracks.

He turns to face me and smiles. "How did you know I was from Ireland?" His accent is strong.

He has Ireland written all over his face, with Dublin at his ear and Cork on his chin, and as my mother noticed the night she met my father at a dance here in Queens, he walks like a farmer. I can always spot an Irish man. They dress a certain way, and they walk a certain way. They even cock their heads and wink like no other men I know.

"Your neck," I tell him. "I can spot an Irish neck miles away."

"Where are you from?" he asks, assuming I was born in Ireland.

"Queens. My parents are Irish."

"What county?"

"Mum is from Donegal, and Dad's family come from Roscommon and Waterford."

"Have you ever been over?"

"Every year since I was a baby."

"So you know it well."

We chat for the remainder of the journey and discover we are both getting out at Times Square to transfer trains. I'm heading uptown, and he is heading downtown. We continue to chat up the escalator and walk in opposite directions when we reach the top, but we are still facing each other.

"What's your name?" he calls as he slowly walks his farmer walk backward. There is a bit of flirtation about him.

"Tara," I respond, smiling as I too walk backward.

"Do you want to get a drink sometime, Tara?" There's the cock of the head and the wink not far behind.

I stop and walk in his direction to hand him my card, which has been in my pocket, ready to jump out of the gate like a horse at Belmont. Success!

My girlfriends do not approve of my stalking, despite the fact that I've gone on two different dates with two different men due to my efforts. They think it's creepy. But I find it easier to talk to someone in transit than in a bar. There is no agenda, or so he thinks. If he doesn't ask for the number, I simply hand it over with a smile. It's flattering for him. But I, as usual, am doing all the work. Men in New York don't do the asking anymore.

As soon as I get into the office, I turn on my computer and send a message to my friend Lauren about the man I met on the train. She advises me to search the missed-connections link on a site called Love on the Underground since, in her words, "it's much safer than stalking, sweetie."

Lauren is a fashion stylist and trainer. We became fast friends when she joined my team last year in preparation for my backup plan in case I got laid off. She keeps up with trends. She's my Gal Friday.

I decide to take her advice and investigate the link, and I read a post from a woman looking for some guy she saw one morning on the subway:

> You got on the C train somewhere in Brooklyn around 8:35. I was wearing a striped dress, navy-blue sweater. We kept exchanging looks. I brushed your arm (yes, intentionally) on my way off the train. Wanna get a drink sometime?

I think this is much more absurd than my stalking. What are the chances of someone going online at the end of the workday, wondering which stranger noticed him or her and wants to date? It's so random.

Dad calls me the One-Date Wonder. I can't take credit for this phenomenon. It is the result of a deterioration of the rituals of society, of traditions lost. I am simply a victim of being born in the wrong decade, in the wrong generation, a generation that holds nothing sacred, from a sunrise to the boiling of an egg, from the stealing of a kiss to the space between a pair of dancers.

In nature, the male of the species uses his instinct. He flaunts his feathers and chases off competitors. He knows what he wants without hesitation. Male crickets risk their lives to protect their females. I can't even get a guy to ask me on a date or offer to buy me a coffee, let alone display inherited traits. The birds and the bees don't require self-help books on dating, nor do they use the internet to find a mate. They simply get out there and do their thing.

I get out there every night of the week to networking events, live performances, restaurants, book stores, the gym, supermarkets, pubs, street fairs, cinemas, workshops, tango classes, subway stations, airports, electronics stores, hot dog stands, sports arenas, and even funerals—just about anywhere I can—to meet a man. I've tried speed dating, eHarmony, Match.com, and blind dates set up by friends and family. I've even written to Oprah and Ellen for their assistance, but they haven't responded yet.

My mother often talks about my single status with her elderly patients. She is a caregiver for seniors who suffer from Alzheimer's disease. One of her patients, Geraldine, was so determined to help me find a man that she made Mom walk with her to Saint Joseph's Church every day, where Geraldine placed a twenty-dollar bill in the donation box. I didn't find a man during her vigil, but Saint Joseph's became wealthy. Geraldine wasn't aware that Saint Joseph is the patron saint of carpenters, fathers, house hunters, travelers, people in doubt, and Canada but not of single women.

Don't get me wrong; it's not like I haven't had significant others. I've had moments that old women's minds travel to as they sit alone on the front porches of their memories and soak up the sultry days of their youth—enough moments to blush the cheeks of a nun, including moments of "I love you" and "I've never met anyone like you." But none amounted to "Will you marry me?" or at least "Will you date me long enough to meet my family?" That's why Dad nicknamed me the One-Date Wonder. Men might date me longer than a song but never the length of an album.

The boys were in abundance when my braces and glasses came off, but as they reluctantly entered their thirties, dating wasn't fun anymore. It became a job interview: "So where did you go to school? What do you do for a living? Where do you see yourself in five years? Which political party do you support? Shall we split the check?"

I suppose some people might call me a late bloomer. When I was eight years old, I wanted to be a writer. I wrote in diaries and journals, on oak tag, on sidewalks with chalk, on napkins at fast-food restaurants—on anything and anywhere to record that I was in a cocoon and not yet ready to spread my glorious wings. I imagined that one day I would morph into a dazzling, colorful creature and fly above the nonsense that surrounded me in the prison called Saint Luke's Elementary School. I was sure to transform into a butterfly when the hibernation of my adolescence was complete. But I knew I wasn't ready. I anticipated a long wait for my metamorphosis. The typical transformation period lasts from a few days to a few months. But I am not typical.

People rarely call each other anymore. Now it's only a brief email or short text: "C U soon. TTYL." Is our time so precious that we can't use it to at least spell out all the words? I miss handwritten letters and full-length correspondence. I miss chatting with Granny Nora on the phone. She wrote letters to me throughout my childhood, and we spoke on the phone every Sunday. Her voice reached to me across the three thousand miles of ocean that divided us during the school year. Hers was the voice that sang to me from her pantry while she fried my morning feed of sausages with tea and toast smothered in Kerry Gold butter and Chivers raspberry jam.

"Deedle-dee-idle-deedle-eye."

Hers was the voice that called to me and Duke, her collie, down the muddy lanes to the fields where we sat propped up against haystacks, daydreaming.

"Tara! Come up for your supper, and bring that dog with ya!"

Her lilting voice had the gift of gathering chickens for a feeding frenzy when her intention was to locate the dog, and vice versa.

"Duke? Duke!" she'd call, and the chickens were at her feet, as they answered to the word *juke.*

"Juuu-ke juke-juke-juke!" She'd call, and the dog would come running. Duke eventually got a name change to Prince.

My grandparents were married for sixty years. I only witnessed twenty-six of those years until my grandfather died, but I've never seen their equal. He always noticed the color of her cardigan. She always tamed a wild hair on his head. They sometimes held hands under the table, and she'd squeal and laugh when he gave her a pinch.

I'd enjoy a pinch under the table, but I only ever seem to get a poke through Facebook. Tweeting and texting are not as titillating as the human touch. I like that some elderly folks don't know how to turn on a computer, so they request that you meet them for a cup of tea and sympathy. Face time is more gratifying than Facebook.

I want to get beyond the surface, under the skin, to the purple moments, to the hand holding, the promise rings, the courage under fire, and the word heard in the flesh, face-to-face, directly in the eyes, the windows of the soul. Everyone is afraid to look, afraid to see and be seen, afraid to dive and swim to the depths of the matter in case they forget how to breathe. I want the electricity to turn on beyond the screen so that a fire of passion burns at the core and a light illuminates the mind's eye, so there will always be hand holding under the table in our eighties and things to talk about at the end of the day.

Where is that champion, I ask you, he who is daring enough to expose his soul, ignore the distractions, and awaken to the possibilities? Not on this island, I'm afraid. Not in my generation.

I need to hit the road soon and find a cowboy where the streets have no name.

6

Strawberry Fields Forever—The Beatles

The atmosphere in the office has changed from anxiety to remorse. We were all waiting for the call, but we didn't know which one of us would get it. Pretty much half the department has been laid off, and the other half are not entirely relieved, as they realize their duties will most likely change to accommodate the losses.

I seem to be the only person skipping down the halls like a schoolgirl at the end of June. I tell myself to contain my elation, as I'm sure others will not find my behavior welcome, nor will they understand it. I'm not sure I fully understand it. I just lost my job. Why am I so damn happy? Perhaps I am excited about the possibilities. I can do anything I want now. I can start fresh. I can imagine a new reality. I'm not married, I don't have children, and I don't have a mortgage. Except the mortgage, these are all things I've always wanted—expected, in fact—but for some reason, they aren't currently in the master plan of the Universe.

So what is my plan now?

My supervisor calls my name from across the hall. I can hear the tension in her voice. Before I get to respond, she and her throbbing nostrils are above me.

Oh Jay-sus, what did I do or not do now?

I never know with this woman. It could be anything from the size of a font I used in a contract to neglecting her plants when she was out of the office.

Although I work in an arts organization, not all of my time is spent designing creative workshops and attending performances (or writing songs on my lunch hour). There are downsides to every job—paperwork, meetings, supervisors.

Earlier this morning, I decided to send off an email to a client requesting information on a budgetary issue. I copied my supervisor because I have learned not to send anything without her knowledge of it. I've also learned to announce when I am going to the ladies' room, just in case she sees my desk chair empty. But as she stands above me using a great deal of body language, I realize why I am so elated that I only have two more weeks in this asylum.

Her voice trembles and rises as she interrogates me. "Why did you send that email? How could you have sent that email? Why couldn't you wait for my approval? Why do you always do this?"

Why, why, why?

I have no answer. I just look at her nostrils and wonder why she is so angry.

Nothing I wrote in the email was inappropriate. It was all professional, in my opinion. The information was correct. So why is she getting so emotional about a budgetary email?

Perhaps it's because she lives alone, doesn't own a cat to keep her company, and can't even keep plants, as she kills them involuntarily. Or maybe it's because she is single, can't get past a second date, eats cold leftovers in front of reruns, and hasn't been hugged in a while. *Wait—that all sounds too much like me.*

Maybe she is just one sandwich short of a picnic. Yes, I decide, she must be mentally unstable.

When she finishes her rant, I look up at her and say I am sorry with no emotion, expression, or meaning because the only thing I am sorry about is the fact that I have to put up with this nonsense for two more weeks. I'm tired of working in an office from nine to five and sitting through three-hour meetings in which we debate the use of the word *aesthetic* in a document, all the while daydreaming about an alternate reality.

When she retreats to her cubicle, I grab my ID and head for the elevator. I need some fresh air. I am opening the emergency exit on this flight to nowhere.

Although the sun is blazing, clouds are forming inside my chest, making my spirit heavy. Maybe I am disgruntled because of the routine or feel confined on subways and in office spaces with people who don't look each other in the eye or say, "Bless you," when you sneeze. Or maybe I just need a hug.

I make my way to Central Park a few short blocks from the office. The trees there have a way of enlightening me, especially along the Literary Walk. I surrender onto an empty bench near a musician playing a saxophone and release a hearty sigh.

My father is a traditional Irish fiddle player. He once told me if you don't play a fiddle, it dies. The wood requires vibration to stay alive. I can relate. My spirit has lost its song, but I feel the skin itching under my blouse.

At the moment of death, some say we are reborn like caterpillars turning into butterflies—transforming, reincarnating. Perhaps we have many deaths in our lives. We shed old skins, learn new tricks, and start over. The soul carries on with or without its skin. Maybe the soul is on a journey. It travels through time and space. It takes the A train, borrows butterfly wings, and hitches rides across the highways of our lives, all by the light of the moon.

I love Central Park. The runners, the lovers, the music makers—they all come to this oasis in each remarkable season, lying on wool blankets under an autumn sun, watching butterflies flitter above benches near spring tulips, and gazing at stars on summer nights where millions have lingered, inhaling the city through a saxophone. The notes fill their nostrils like honey-roasted peanuts. The trees, naked in winter, exposed, with icicles replacing leaves, display their strength, waiting patiently, silently, until spring, when they are reborn, transformed, like the city each day, each hour, each New York minute.

Do trees hold memories? I wonder as I stare up at the tall trunks competing with skyscrapers. *Can they hear our laughter? Share our sorrows? Or do they simply stand and observe like the NYPD in the subway station at Times Square?* These trees have spied on the first of a million kisses. Their leaves have been collected for second-grade science projects. Children have climbed their limbs, as I did, to watch their fathers and mothers run the New York City Marathon from branches that could not carry the full weight of their seven-year-old bodies. *Does that tree remember dropping me?*

Other trees are more inviting, craving the spotlight, such as those accessorized with Chinese lanterns adorning their leaves at Tavern on the Green, overlooking tea service with cucumber sandwiches and scones with raspberry preserves and clotted cream, and those wearing sparkling white lights to compete with the diamonds adorning the lobes and necklines of members of the Film Society at Lincoln Center, eavesdropping on gossip from the rich and not so famous.

I imagine these trees are the reincarnated spirits of former New Yorkers. Who was the weeping willow? The dogwood? The pine? Could the European beech be an ancestor of mine? Will I be an oak or a cedar when I die? I aspire to be an American elm towering over the Literary Walk, creating a canopy of crimson in autumn and scribbling shadows on the pavement with my branches like the doodling of an author's hand, a sonnet by Shakespeare, a poem by Robert Burns. The mighty, majestic American elm has arms that bend like a yogini from the New York Sports Club and is as elegant and graceful as a ballerina from the State Theater. Elms line the walk like VIPs in the front row of a fashion show, observing the styles of the passersby.

A United Nations of trees share this urban forest—Japanese crabapples, Turkish filberts, Spanish oaks.

A feast of trees are sprinkled through the park like seasonings for the most finicky foodie, from cherry to chestnut and mulberry to maple.

There is even a tree above the Wollman ice-skating rink called the Tree of Heaven. Perhaps New Yorkers don't go to heaven when they die. They rest eternally in Central Park, near the Boathouse, overlooking the Strawberry Fields memorial, on the Great Lawn, or near the Jackie Onassis Reservoir. Generation after generation, people picnic at their roots, carve hearts into their trunks, and give them an occasional hug inspired by intoxication or love as they wonder, reflect, imagine, and dream.

If only I could sit here all day, listening to the music from the saxophone, feeling the sun on my face, and pondering the past lives of trees. But I have to return to the mental ward where no one says, "Good morning," or "Bless you" when you sneeze. I'm not complaining. As Granny Nora used to say, "Sure, I'd have no one to listen to me."

I'd love to jump into a car and just go somewhere—anywhere. I want to disturb the landscape of a sacred place with the rear wheels of a fast car or take a back road where the skies are not cloudy all day.

I rise with reluctance and wink at the trees with a promise to return soon.

When the light turns green, I make my way across Columbus Avenue to return to the office. Then it happens—or almost happens: my near-death experience.

As I approach the middle of the intersection, I catch a glimpse of a marigold bull out of the corner of my eye. He barrels into my legs, and like a matador, I move with the beast's enormous frame so as not to get hurt. I hear the gasps of horror from the crowded Plaza de Toros as the marigold bull tosses me up into the air as if in slow motion. I roll onto his long, wide frame like a flamenco dancer and feel the heat he emits from his metal nostrils. His horn pierces my ears.

That's when I realize I am not in Seville but on the street in Manhattan, on the hood of a yellow taxi. I slide down off the hood and onto the pavement as adrenaline rushes into my limbs.

"What the fuck is wrong with you?" I scream at the driver as I slam my hand down on his car with full homage to Dustin Hoffman in *Midnight Cowboy*. "I'm walkin' here!" I notice his two passengers cower in the backseat.

"I'm sorry, love. I didn't see you." He has an English accent—southeast London, to be exact. It startles me, and I stare at him, wondering why, of all the taxi drivers in all of New York City, the one who hits me is English. What are the odds? I've heard Jamaican accents, Indian accents, Russian accents, and Ghanaian accents but never English.

I resume my rant. "Well, open your fucking eyes, asshole!" Curses usually only leave my mouth when I stub my toe.

Pedestrians gather and ask if I'm all right. Everyone is looking. We bring traffic to a standstill. I feel self-conscious and continue to cross the street, leaving the scene of the accident. My legs melt on the sidewalk, and when I finally register what has happened, I start to cry. I limp back to the office, back up the elevator, and back to my desk, where I find my coworkers quietly typing away without having noticed my return.

I sit down and say through my tears, "I was just hit by a taxi."

My cardigan-wearing coworker turns around and rolls his swivel chair toward me without getting up from his seat. My supervisor crosses the hall immediately. They question me as others gather to see what the commotion is all about.

"Oh my God, are you all right?"

"Are you hurt?"

"Did you get his license?"

"How did it happen?"

"We didn't even know you were gone."

7

London Calling—The Clash

As I think of the English accent of the driver who almost killed me on Columbus Avenue, I wonder if Granny Nora had anything to do with my not being seriously injured by the taxi. I must have a guardian angel protecting me or a spirit guide sending me messages. There's always a sign—like "The Sound of Music" in the subway to lift my mood the other morning or the rooster in the snowstorm to ease my anxiety last winter. Someone or something is always with me, just like when I fulfilled Granny Nora's last wish. She told me she had always wanted to return to London, where she lived for four years as a young woman. I returned on her behalf one November a few years after she died.

The late-afternoon sun was retreating behind a row of conservatively attached houses. I stood in front of number eleven on Garden Road. As I reached for the doorbell, my hand shook—and not because of the cold.

My Austrian friend Florian had graciously accompanied me on the unusual excursion. He stood behind me.

"You're not going in, are you?" he asked as I looked at him and pressed the buzzer.

We waited. Florian squinted, looking up the narrow street with his hands tucked away in his pockets. Suddenly, a white image appeared behind the kaleidoscope of glass panes, and the door swung open.

When I'd informed my friends back in New York that I was going to London to see the house my grandmother lived in during the 1930s, they all had asked if my family still lived in that house. I'd replied no, as if that were of any consequence. Bewildered, they'd inquired further with confused expressions. "Well then," they'd asked, "whom do you expect to find living there?"

"Probably an Indian family," I'd said, "since there is a large Indian population in London. Perhaps some woman with a sari and a red dot on her forehead will answer the door."

As the door swung open, there she stood, the Indian woman with her white sari, but the red dot—or bindi, as it is properly called—was not on her forehead. The only reason I didn't laugh was because I was fighting back tears. I tried to hurry through my introduction so that I didn't begin crying on the Indian woman's front steps.

"I know you might think I'm crazy," I said with a forced smile, "but my grandmother lived in this house back in 1939, and I just traveled three thousand miles to see it."

I paused and expected the woman to slam the door in my face. At first glance, she most likely assumed we were lost, selling something, or even preaching door-to-door, as it was a Sunday afternoon. But her soft, round face broke into a warm, inviting smile that reminded me of my mother's. In an instant, she recognized a family duty, a bond linking generations, the quest of a granddaughter. She widened the door and stepped aside to let us into her home.

"Welcome! Welcome! Come. Come inside! Very cold outside."

"Really?" I asked in astonishment, my heart dancing.

I looked to my friend, who was cautiously shaking his head, but I encouraged him with a pleading nod. I hadn't come all that way to stand in the street and take photos like a tourist.

I was staying at Florian's flat with his girlfriend near Kensington Palace. We'd been friends since high school. He'd agreed to escort me to that part of town as his only tour-guiding duty. It was a bit far from Kensington Palace, and it didn't help that the tube was on fire most of the afternoon. That fiasco had altered the direct route he had initially navigated for us. We could have been to Vienna and back in the time it took us to get to the stop on the Brown Line north of the city center—Bakerloo, it was called.

As we entered the narrow hall, my eyes ran up a steep carpeted staircase. I wondered what had been altered in the house and what remained the same. The wallpaper looked as though it were the original. I imagined my granny standing in that hall and adjusting her hat in front of the mirror. She'd always liked to look her best.

"Would you like a cup of tea or some homemade curry? Do you like curry? Indian curry. Very good," the woman said as she invited us into her home.

"Oh no, thank you. That's so kind of you." I was still in disbelief that I was actually inside the house. "Are you sure this is okay?"

"Oh yes. Yes, very okay. Please sit. Sit." She repeated everything twice.

The lady in the white sari led us into her sitting room off to the right of the hall. A young woman entered the room. She was dressed in a lovely lavender sari, and I noticed a French manicure. She stopped abruptly and examined our foreign faces. Although Florian is Austrian, he looks more like a Mediterranean man than a member of the Von Trapp family. The Indian woman introduced the young woman as her daughter. The mother repeated the reason for our visit with great enthusiasm. The daughter greeted us politely, but I could tell our intrusion had disturbed their afternoon tea. She looked as though she were questioning her mother's sanity: *How can you be so naive and let these foreign invaders into our home? How can we believe they are who they say they are?*

A young man entered the room from a door behind the couch where the women were now sitting. He had no shirt on and was towel-drying his hair. I'm sure he was aware of our arrival, as he didn't look surprised. He approached the couch like a pit bull.

"Ere's my bruhvah," the young woman said. The daughter's

accent was different from her mother's. She obviously had been raised in London.

Her brother nodded and remained standing while continuing to dry his already dry skin.

During the brief introductions, the mother didn't remove the smile from her round face. It was genuine. She was delighted, as if she'd been expecting us. I wanted her and her adult children to understand why I was there in their sitting room. I also wanted to take off my warm coat, as the house was approximately 128 degrees Fahrenheit, but I didn't want them to think I was moving in, so I keep it on. Florian hadn't removed his uncomfortable expression.

I began to explain with a rather goofy expression that my grandmother had lived in that house when she moved from Ireland at the age of seventeen. "She took care of seven of her eleven siblings in this house. She spent four years here in London and all the while dated my grandfather, whom she initially met back in Ireland. He worked in another part of England, but they wrote letters to each other and went out on weekends to dances."

The brother and sister stared blankly at me. At times, a hint of suspicion crossed one of their faces but never in unison. Their mother was radiant and all ears. She urged me to continue with my story.

"My grandparents had their wedding party in this house," I told them. "It was a double wedding. Granny's brother, Michael, married his wife on the very same day. The pair of newlyweds walked down the aisle together. The church was supposed to be in this neighborhood. She said her mother posted twenty-one chickens in the mail for the wedding feast."

"Chickens in the mail?" the mother asked as she looked in disbelief from me to her son and daughter. "Were they dead or alive?"

"That's exactly what I asked my granny!" I exclaimed.

Granny had roared with laughter when I asked her the same question the summer before she passed. "Obviously the chickens were dead!" she'd crowed. "How could someone put live chickens in the mail? They had to be bled first." But of course. Every New Yorker knows that.

The Indian mother shook with laughter, but her children still did not find me amusing.

Then I said the magic words: "There was a pear tree in the back garden."

My welcome mat was finally uncovered. The daughter's face lit up with recognition. She leaped off the couch, took my hand in hers, and led me down the narrow hall and out through the curry kitchen to the back garden. There she pointed to a tree beside the house.

"But this is an apple tree," I said as I stood with the daughter in the otherwise barren garden.

Florian and the mother joined us outside under the November sky.

The daughter smiled and said, "We cut down that bloody pear tree a few years ago. Mum prefers apples."

Granny had made a lovely dessert with the pears—after cooking the dead chickens that were mailed from Ireland.

I was no longer a stranger. They believed I was who I said I was. My family had lived in that house. They'd broken bread, danced, procreated, and prayed in that house, just as the Indian family did. I'd come from New York to see a house my grandmother and her brothers and husband had lived in for four short years. It was just a house, with brick walls, a kitchen now filled with the smells of curry, a sitting room, bedrooms upstairs, and a tree that bore fruit in the back garden. There was not much history there, but it was still a piece of my history. My grandparents married in the church down the street. They hosted parties in the French room. They ate lots of juicy pears.

But soon after the May wedding, the honeymooners had to evacuate the city. It was 1939. They had two choices: remain in London, with its city streets and proper sidewalks, risking their lives while my grandfather fought for England, or return to Ireland to a life of waking before the sun to milk the cows, work the land, and pray to God. They left the city on August 24, one week before Hitler invaded Poland.

If it weren't for the war, I wouldn't be alive today. It's an odd thing to say—actually downright insensitive. But if the Germans hadn't been threatening most of Europe, my grandparents would have remained in England and raised my mother there. They instead moved back to Ireland to the safety of their potato fields, where my mother was born. Mom eventually left Ireland at the age of seventeen to find work in America. Her migration led her to meet my father in New York, and that's where she gave birth to me and my brother, Tommy. Everyone's path of migration affects everyone else's.

Granny gave me the address of the house in London two months before she died. She had never spoken about it before, or perhaps I wasn't listening. She told me how she longed to revisit London and her house one day just to see it again. I didn't realize when she said it that it was one of her last wishes.

We returned to the Indian family's sitting room, where I welcomed the warmth. Although both women were now smiling, we all sat in silence. Florian continued to look uncomfortable, but he politely smiled back at them. I knew he was thinking we had overstayed our welcome and should not have resumed our position on the couch, but I didn't want to leave yet. I needed to absorb the moment. I'd come that far. I needed to see what she could not see. I'd come for her. It was her last wish. There were doors I hadn't opened, nooks I hadn't investigated, and drawers I hadn't rummaged through in search for something. But what? So we continued to sit in an awkward silence.

I looked at the bedsheets covering the couches to protect them from dust and body oils. A calendar from a local business was hanging above one of the couches. Artificial flowers sat in a basket next to a ceramic swan. The television was wedged into a corner between the front window and the fireplace. The bookshelves were cluttered with books, magazines, and picture frames. The smell of curry continued to accent the room. It was a cozy home.

Then it happened—what I'd been waiting for: a sign. Above the awkward silence, I heard it. It was subtle at first, but it grew louder and louder, like the violin singing in the Times Square subway station, like the rooster crowing in the snowstorm, reminding me of one of my favorite Edgar Allan Poe short stories, wherein the beating of a murdered man's heart under the floorboards grows louder and louder as the murderer stands before the police, hoping they don't hear it as well. I looked up above the mantel and pointed. The mother raised her eyebrows and followed my finger.

"Oh, the clock?" she said.

"Yes. My grandparents' house in Ireland was very quiet at times. All one could hear was the crackling of the fire or the dog barking at a passing car. So the ticking of a clock always makes me think of the pair of them in their quiet cottage."

We all sat attentively and listened to the clock ticking on the wall. It began to fill the room. It almost became deafening. *Ticktock. TICK-TOCK.* The mother breathed in deeply, laid her hand on her chest, and let out a long sigh. She turned to me and smiled.

"She is here with us," she said as my throat tightened. "Spirits have a way of letting us know they are present."

The daughter rolled her eyes. "Mum, what the bloody 'ell you goin' on about? It's a bleedin' clock."

"Oh, they think I am old fashioned," she said, dismissing her daughter. "Yes, yes, but I know what I am saying. Her spirit is here, and she is very, very happy you brought her back to see her house one last time. Very happy indeed."

I felt chicken pimples—Florian's phrase for goose bumps—form on my arms. I smiled at the lovely Indian mother and then looked at the time on the ticking clock: 3:50 p.m. I realized I had gotten what I came for, and now it was time to go. I thanked the mother for her generosity and kindness. I warned her that a few more strangers might visit one day if my mother and her sisters ever got the courage to come see the house as well. She let me take a photo of her and her daughter. I hadn't noticed when or to where the son had disappeared. We said our farewells, and Florian and I were on the street again in the fresh, crisp autumn air. Florian was relieved to be outside.

As we walked down the street, I looked back at the house. I imagined Garden Road lined with vintage cars. I thought of my grandmother walking along the sidewalk. I followed her footsteps to a church a few blocks up from the house.

Saint Joseph's Catholic Church stood tall at the top of the road. It bares the same saint's name as the church my mother visited daily with her patient Geraldine. I asked Florian to take a few photos of me outside, like a tourist, and then, just as we entered the church, the bells began to toll. It was four o'clock. For the second time that day, I felt chicken pimples. Without planning on it, I'd arrived in the church where my grandparents had married, at precisely the hour they'd wed. Now I knew she was with me.

I dipped my finger into the holy water just to the right of the entrance, made the sign of the cross, and walked over to light a candle under a statue of the Virgin Mary. Florian went off in the opposite direction to give me a moment. I placed a coin in the donation box and chose a candle to light in the second row of votives. With my eyes closed, I released a sigh and searched for a prayer.

"What did you whisper to me the day you died?" I waited. No response. "Okay. Fine. You did it, Granny. You got me into a church."

I hadn't set foot in a church since her funeral mass.

"Now all you have to do is help me find my dance partner. Where is he? Don't you have a bird's-eye view up there?"

Every time I think of my single status, I notice a pair of birds land on a nearby fence or directly on the sidewalk in front of me. This is either pure coincidence, or I'm starring in my own animated Disney film. When I see these birds, I can't help but think of my grandparents. It's as if they are tweeting, "Don't worry. We're with you. Everything will turn out all right."

But I've given up hope on finding love. Granny Nora always prayed for me every morning and every night. Who is praying for me now? How will I ever find a man in today's society without Divine intervention?

8

Let's Get away from It All—Frank Sinatra

The executive director says I can go home early because I have been hit by a taxi. I decide I should leave early. I'm desperate to get out of this office anyway. I make my way to the subway, looking both ways as I cross the street—twice, just to make sure. But I don't go home. I meet Lauren for a chat 'n' chew at our favorite cupcake, beer, and wine bar down on Carmine Street. I'm still shaken from my experience, I don't want to be alone, and there's nothing like artisan cupcakes to help you forget your troubles.

"So what happened, sweetie?" Lauren pulls me into a warm embrace before we settle down to the serious business of choosing our cupcakes.

It is not a coincidence that she picked a place to decompress that was born out of the inspiration of a layoff. The owner was a businesswoman climbing the ladder of success, when she was suddenly pushed off and decided to get her revenge by opening the most delicious location in town.

"This has just been a crazy few days," I say as I slump into my chair.

"I know! A layoff, a potential date with a guy you stalked on the subway, and now getting hit by a taxi. You just refuse to lead a boring life." She smiles at me. Her pale face is glowing.

"I forgot about the date. He hasn't called anyway." I look at my phone to see if there are any messages from the Irish guy.

A waitress brings a few menus, and Lauren thanks her.

"But you are okay? I mean, you don't need to go to a hospital or anything?" She looks concerned.

"I just need a cupcake. Death by chocolate is really the only way to go." I look down at the menu.

"What do you fancy?" she asks, drooling over the menu.

"I think I want the Dirty cupcake this time. But only if you get the Crimson and Cream so we can share," I say.

The menu pairs the most orgasmic cupcakes with beers and wines from all over the world. I could order a Kopparberg pear cider from Sweden with my Valrhona dark chocolate truffle cupcake, but I order a cup of herbal pear tea. I rarely see pear on a menu, and it reminds me of Granny Nora's pear tree in her London garden. Again, it feels like a sign that she is with me.

"So what are you going to do?" Lauren asks as the waitress walks away with our orders.

"I'm going to eat a cupcake," I respond dryly.

"I mean after that, silly. What's the plan?"

"I don't know." I look at her as she pulls a loose strand of her red hair behind her ear, and I remember the photograph of my father's mother, with her red hair and the look of wanderlust in her Irish eyes. "But I think I need to do this road trip."

Lauren claps her hands like an excited child. "Have you figured out how, and more importantly, do I get to come with you?"

I laugh as I take a sip of water. "I've been wondering—what if I could take a 1957 Chevy Bel Air across the country and go to all the places my dad's mother went on her road trip? I never met her. I know nothing about her, actually, except that she took this extraordinary journey before she died. It would be a way for me to get to know her. Maybe she's the reason why I've always had this desire to drive across country."

"That sounds amazing! So what's stopping you?"

"Well, I don't know anyone who owns that particular vintage car, nor would they want me to put six thousand miles on it." I bite my lip and stare out the window.

"Why don't you rent one?"

"I've searched a few sites. They pretty much only rent them for local weddings or movie shoots. And they are ridiculously expensive."

The waitress brings our decadent treats. We greet them with juvenile excitement and take pictures of our gorgeous food with our phones before we dig in. The flavors are truly inspiring.

"Well, whatever you decide to do," Lauren manages to say through her mouthful, "I'm going with you. My schedule is flexible, and I'm looking for a change myself."

I smile at her, not only because she looks so funny stuffing her face with red velvet cake but also because she has really been there for me these past few years, even while she was going through a divorce.

We met at a mutual friend's live performance, where I learned that she is a fashion stylist, and she learned that I am a jazz singer. Both of our passions are on the side. My family encourages creativity but only if practiced part-time. They are always going on about getting a "real job."

In our full-time gigs, Lauren is a gym trainer by day, and I am—or was or will soon no longer be—a program manager at a prestigious arts education organization. We both prefer our passions on the side, but neither passion pays the rent.

One day in the office, a visiting jazz musician heard me singing to myself and complimented my vocal styling. I took advantage of the moment and bragged that I could sing "Danny Boy" like Billie Holiday. He said he didn't know Lady Day had recorded the famous Irish song. I laughed and explained that she hadn't recorded the song, but I could imitate her intonation. When he requested proof, I performed the song for him a cappella. His eyes lit up like lightbulbs, and he said I should record my version of that song. I laughed off the idea and joked that I could record an entire album of traditional Irish songs but swing them like Billie Holiday or Ella Fitzgerald.

"Now, that's an idea," he said to me with certainty in the creases of his mouth. Then we watched the idea float above our heads as the lingering notes of my spontaneous performance mingled with his words of possibility.

Talk of cutbacks and layoffs was already in the air in the office. We knew the storm was coming, and the new idea of my recording old Irish songs was percolating like the coffee that would soon disappear from the office pantry. As I rode the subway each morning, I arranged different traditional Irish songs in my head, imagining how they would sound as swing, jazz, or blues. I could hear the saxophone breathe in "Black Velvet Band," and I could hear a trumpet cry in "Danny Boy."

"I'll Tell Me Ma" had a natural swinging rhythm to it. Granny Nora used to sing that to me in her kitchen in Donegal: "I'll tell me ma when I go home the boys won't leave the girls alone; they pull my hair and stole my comb, but that's all right till I go home. She is handsome. She is pretty. She is the belle of ..." *New York City? I think this can work*, I told myself.

I called Lauren after I set a date for my band in a recording studio downtown. She arranged to conduct the photo shoot for the album cover on the same day I recorded the tracks. We both enjoy multitasking. Before the big day, she took me shopping for the wardrobe and borrowed vintage accessories from designers. She also got permission to use a historic landmark building in Midtown where she had connections. It's always about connections.

In one day, I recorded my first album and had my first professional photo shoot. I felt like a bride on her wedding day with all the activity and attention. It was an exhausting but deliriously fun fifteen-hour day, a dream fulfilled. I had always wanted to record an album. It was on my extended list of "Things I've Always Wanted to Do." It was also my backup plan in case I got laid off. I figured if I could start selling CDs and begin my music career before I lost my job, at least I'd have a foot in the door of a different industry. I couldn't have done it without my Gal Friday.

When we put ideas out into the Universe, things happen. I've learned over the years that when I think positive thoughts or write things down on Post-it notes, they become reality. It's that whole if-you-build-it philosophy from the movie *Field of Dreams* with Kevin Costner. I didn't fully understand the power of thoughts or words until the past few years, when those thoughts and words became tangible. It's rather mind-boggling. But when we hold the result of our dreams and ideas in our hands, like a freshly self-produced CD in a shiny jacket, it's empowering.

Perhaps this explains why, though I was laid off this week, I am not as disgruntled as most people are when they lose their jobs. I have a backup plan in place. However, the music business is a tricky one, and even though the songs I recorded, the very ones Granny Nora sang to me in her kitchen, are now being played on Irish radio and even jazz stations across the globe, the money and job offers are not exactly pouring in just yet. Besides, I have other things on my mind, like taking this cross-country road trip.

Lauren and I finish our decadent cupcakes and buy a few more for the road, as we didn't eat dinner yet. Evening suddenly surprises us with its shadows and dimly lit streetlamps as dusk enters downtown.

"You will always be my copilot," I tell her as I wrap my arms around her neck.

"Like Thelma and Louise!" She giggles and gives me another squeeze.

"But I get to be Thelma." I point my finger at her. "Because she's the one who ends up with Brad Pitt."

"Hey, that's not fair." She playfully swings her arm at me.

"Wait—we have the same initials! Tara and Lauren. Thelma and Louise. It's only natural that I get Brad." I beam at her.

"We can both search for our Brad Pitt," Lauren says.

"But we won't die in the end. Let's just stay away from the Grand Canyon," I add as I walk toward the subway.

"Oh my, you are too much. Good night, sweetie. Safe home!" she calls as I watch her red hair dance down Bedford in the dark.

9

Moon River—Audrey Hepburn

I don't like taking the subway home late at night. More crimes happen in my neighborhood after dark, around the witching hour. But I can't afford a taxi, and besides, the train is just as crowded at midnight as it is at rush hour.

I always wonder where all these people come from at all hours of the day and night. Were they selling fake Gucci bags on Canal Street? Washing floors in some hip new restaurant in SoHo where the customers don't speak their language? Performing traditional songs in subway stations as commuters ignored their melodies of heartache and homesickness? How can I ever be afraid on the International Express, when everyone is exhausted from chasing the American dream?

The train pulls into Queensboro Plaza, and a mass pushes their way out as another mass pushes their way in like salmon. In only four more stops, I can run the two blocks to my safe little apartment next to the Boulevard of Death.

"Hey! Don't fucking push me!" a woman's voice shouts above the already quiet subway car of sleepy immigrants.

Oh, here we go, I say to myself.

"Don' shuff me!" I hear a man respond.

I look to my right and see a large Caucasian woman, brawny like an all-American football player, towering over an Asian man.

"You fuckin' touched me! Don't touch me, you fuckin' Chink!"

Seriously? She has no class, but she has the attention of the entire subway car. The drama escalates.

"Don' call me Chink! I no Chinese!" The man is insulted that she can't tell the difference.

"I don't care what you are, you stupid minority! Go back to your own fuckin' country!"

No one says anything, except for the train as it rumbles and mumbles above the sleepy rhythm of the tracks. Passengers simply stare as if they are watching late-night television.

"You white trash!" the man says to her in anger.

"Kneel before me!" she responds with her face right up to his.

She is degrading and ignorant, and I want to shut her up, but there are twenty people between us, and I'm afraid she'll tell me to kneel before her too. Doesn't she realize we are the minorities on this train? She and I are the only white women in the entire subway car. Everyone else was born in Asia, Central America, South America, or the Caribbean.

Your worth is determined by your service to others.

These words came to me in a recent dream, waking me from a deep sleep. I jumped up from bed to write them down on a piece of paper in the dark.

Is that what Granny Nora whispered to me on the day she died?

Then the man socks it to her, not with his fist but with his words, and I wish he'd been on my debate team in high school—that is, if I'd been on a debate team, which I wasn't. I feel like doing the wave or cheering. *Yeah, man, you tell her. You put her in her place!*

"Who's in the White House?" he says to her, and the audience finally perks up, giving each other approving glances, taking sides more visibly.

"I'll fuckin' kill you!" she says.

"Who's in the White House?" he repeats with more confidence, realizing she has nothing intelligent to come back with.

O'Bama, I sing to myself, proud of his Irish roots in Moneygall, County Offaly.

Then she gives him the blow that will shut him down, and fear takes over his countenance.

"Who do you think the police will side with?" She snickers.

She's a white woman, and he's an immigrant who may or may not be legal. He doesn't want a confrontation. He was minding his own business, taking the subway home from a fifteen-hour shift. He's tired of his job, tired of being put down, and afraid to be sent back to his home country, where he might have less than he has here. So she wins the verbal fight and takes his dignity off the train as she exits with her middle finger extended.

I follow her out because it's also my stop, and I want to trip her down the stairs. I want to spit at her and tell her she has no class and no empathy, and who the hell does she think she is, treating someone like that?

So what? You got pushed on a crowded train. Get over it, lady. This is New York. Move to Montana if you don't want to touch anyone!

But I don't speak to her. She's bigger than I am, and I don't like confrontations. She's already in an aggressive state, and my words would pass over her like the clouds she doesn't notice on a daily basis because she is sleepwalking through her life, unconscious to everything around her unless it gets in her way.

As I race up the sidewalk to escape the dark shadows, I look up at the moon. It's a clear night, with not a cloud in the June sky. The moon is so big and close I want to reach up and grab it. My mind takes me back to Ireland, to a November night when a similar moon ornamented the sky.

One year, my mother took me to Donegal during Thanksgiving week. It was the first time I missed my favorite American holiday. After my grandparents went to bed, I stepped outside their cottage to look at the moon because it was creating the most dramatic shadows in front of the house. I'd never seen a moon like that before. It illuminated the Atlantic like a disco ball. It was the only source of light for miles. It was magical the way it played with the hedges and haystacks. I wanted to remember that moon, so I composed a little poem that night under its spell:

November night so cold so bright,
So clear and clean and free.
Full moon screams white as my ears ache
To hear the silent sea.

With no wind blowing, dogs barking, roosters crowing, or tractors coming up the dirt lane, the land was silent, and the waves cooperated too.

My mother joined me under the moon.

"What are you doing out here in the cold? I thought you were in bed." She was always concerned about me.

"Look at that moon." I directed her attention to the night sky.

"Wow."

"Listen."

"What?"

"Can you hear it?"

"Hear what?"

"Exactly. Nothing," I whispered as we stood and listened to the moon screaming white over the silent sea.

After a long minute or two, her voice broke the silence. "Is that the same moon we see in New York?"

I looked at her and wondered what kind of education the Irish school system had provided before she left Ireland. But I held my disrespectful tongue and answered.

"Yes, it is the same moon."

"Then why does it look so different?" she asked.

I didn't know. We stood there for a few more moments, taking in as much as our senses permitted. It was a moment to notice and absorb. It was a moment I will remember forever, standing under the gaze of that luminous moon, the same November moon that lit the path of the ship that took my mother to America and the same November moon I stood under during my first kiss. There is something magical about the November moon, more so than the honeyed moon in June.

When I finally get safely inside my tiny apartment next to the Boulevard of Death, I carefully place my dinner of cupcakes on the kitchen table and begin to make a cup of tea as I call my parents' number. I haven't spoken to them all day, and I want to hear their voices. They aren't aware of my near-death experience, and I'm not sure if I should upset them.

"Hellooo?" my mom sings into the receiver, recognizing my number.

"Hey, Mama." I sigh, relieved to hear her voice.

"You sound tired. You okay?"

"Yeah, just making a cup of tea."

"So am I, but I like your tea better for some reason. Granny always said you made the best cup of tea."

I imagine my mom sitting at her kitchen table and sipping her tea from a cup with a rooster printed on its side.

Mom's kitchen in Queens is her workshop. It gets a lot of use. It produces freshly baked scones, sometimes on a daily basis. There is no longer a kettle to boil water. That takes too long. Tea is made from the instant water heater next to Dad's coffee maker. Both sit on the counter next to the dish drainer. There are never dishes in the dish drainer. They all go immediately into the dishwasher. If one were to open a cupboard, one would find the most-used recipes taped onto the inside of each door. She has learned a lot of recipes in her fifty years in America. Ingredients clutter the shelves in cupboards above the stove: flour in large Tupperware containers, baking soda, salt, pepper, boxes of raisins, Irish oatmeal, Italian olive oil, spaghetti, bow-tie pasta, and penne pasta but never tomato sauce in a jar. Fresh tomatoes sit on a counter, in a basket weaved by her Donegal father. A drawer is filled with thyme, oregano, cumin, basil leaves, cinnamon, vanilla extract, and birthday candles. Another drawer is cluttered with pennies, pens, paper clips, Post-it notes, old buttons, and a thread and needle. A television sits next to the stovetop and is sometimes splattered with cooking grease. The refrigerator is somewhere under the collage of photos of grandchildren, children, and her house in Ireland. There are also newspaper clippings from *Women's Day* or the *New York Times* about health issues, marriage, or new recipes, held by magnets. There may even be a prayer card of a friend or neighbor who is recently deceased. A small wooden table and set of wooden chairs sit in the center of the tiny kitchen, made by my father in his workshop in the basement. They sit under a ceiling fan and a skylight window he installed to let more light into the kitchen.

Then there are the roosters. There is a rooster clock hanging on the wall next to the fridge. Rooster paintings hang on the opposite wall above the radiator. Rooster decals are displayed high on the walls, just below the ceiling. Plates and platters with depictions of roosters rest above the sliding glass doors. Tea cozies and salt and pepper shakers in the shape of roosters sit on top of the fridge. The magnets holding the photos and newspaper clippings are also roosters. The dishtowels hanging from the door handles under the sink and on the oven door have roosters on them. Inside the cupboards above the dishwasher, the teacups and plates all display rooster prints. The napkins and napkin holders, floor mats, and decals on the sliding glass doors—which are to prevent people, including Mom, from walking right through the glass—all have roosters on them.

A neighbor's child once came into the house and noticed the rooster obsession. She diligently opened every nook and cranny and counted ninety-two roosters on the main floor of the house, from the kitchen, through the dining room, and into the living room. The living room contains lifelike replicas of roosters made out of feathers and foam. One can't help but notice this creature on every detail in the house, including the Christmas ornaments. My father's objections to each newly purchased artifact go unheard.

This obsession began when Granny Nora had to have her rogue rooster in Ireland put down. It attacked her one too many times with its sharp spurs and drew blood around her ankles. There is no room for an aggressive male when it is the hen that rules the house.

The rooster was our daily alarm clock and awakened us to each new day on the farm in Donegal. Despite his violent actions, we missed his morning call and general presence when we returned the following summer. Mom resurrected the rooster in her house in Queens. It has become, for her, a symbol representing everything she has lost from her homeland, including her mother.

The night before my mother left her farm in Donegal at the age of seventeen, she sat in front of the fire, watching her father slowly polish his Sunday shoes with his thick, strong farmer's hands. She had helped those hands pick hundreds of potatoes down the field. She hated picking potatoes. It was a tiresome chore. She'd taught herself to focus on the few feet in front of her and not the rows and rows ahead of her. She almost suggested she delay her departure to assist in picking potatoes with her father the next day—and the next and the next.

She walked outside her parents' cottage to hide the tears that began to form on her face. She looked up at the November moon. It lit up the night sky. The reflection on the ocean made the Atlantic glow. Soon she would be crossing that moonlit ocean, which would take her three thousand miles from the farm, her cottage, and her beloved family. Her uncle in Brooklyn had sent letter after letter requesting that his niece come to America, where she could have a better life. "Sure there's no future for her in Ireland," he wrote.

My teenage mother turned to the shed and watched her shadow stretch down the lane as she headed to the outhouse. Suddenly, she heard a familiar sound: her mother's voice, carried by the wind, landed on her ears like a knife. My mother leaned against the whitewashed wall of the byre and listened to her mother sing as she milked her cows.

How could she be singing, she thought to herself, *when her oldest daughter is about to be hauled off to a foreign land in a ship that might as well be her coffin?*

But Granny always tried to sing herself happy. She'd chase away the sadness of the day with a song. It was the only way she knew to keep her spirits up besides prayer.

In the morning, Granny said farewell to her oldest daughter at the door of the thatched cottage. A cloud hung over everyone's head. Mom's younger brother, Manus, couldn't handle the storm and ran away to hide down in the fields until she left.

It was a downpour of tears, the first of a hundred farewells. With each farewell, Granny relived the first, when her seventeen-year-old daughter Mary got in a car with her father and their cousin Bernard, the father of eighteen children, who'd offered to drive my mother and grandfather down to Cork, where, my mother silently prayed her father would beg her to get back in the car to return to the farm and forget about the nonsense of going to America. But Granddad lost his words, and his Mary boarded a ship that took her three thousand miles away to America, the land of Elvis Presley and the unfamiliar.

My mother wrote a letter to her parents on the ship that took her to New York Harbor. I found it in Granny's house one summer. It is dated Monday, November 11, 1957. November 11 is the exact date of my first kiss, a detail recorded in a diary I received for my thirteenth birthday.

My mother's seventeen-year-old handwriting is surprisingly legible. She wrote that the sea was rough, and she and her friends from school, Brigid and Rosie, didn't eat a bit of food for the first three days of the journey due to their seasickness. She swore she'd never go by ship again. She wrote of the entertainments on the ship, dances and films, and said the three girls went everywhere together.

Brigid and Rosie had a cabin to themselves, but my mother's roommate was an African woman. None of the sheltered young Irish girls had ever seen a person of color before, and most of their friends and family from their small, superstitious town feared the unknown. My mother's country-girl fears forced her to sleep on the floor of Brigid and Rosie's cabin rather than share her own cabin with the curious but beautiful woman whose skin was the color of the loving turf her father used to heat their cottage. Fear often prevents us from seeing the natural warmth behind another person's eyes.

It didn't take my mother long to encounter every color of the rainbow when she landed in New York, and her country-girl fears dissolved into the melting pot of the city she began to call home. Her American wake became more of an awakening when she eventually realized we are all the same under the temporary disguise of our skin because at our core is a brightly burning soul ready to love.

"Mom?" I speak into the phone between sips of my tea.

"Yes, dear?"

"I miss Granny."

"Oh God, so do I. What made you say that?"

I pause for a sip. "I think her spirit was with me today." I can hear the English taxi driver's voice again.

Mom sighs into the receiver. "I always feel that she's with me."

"But what about Dad's mom?" I say.

"What about her?"

"Well, I know nothing about her. I never met her, so I feel I have no connection to her. But Granny Nora—she goes out of her way to make her presence known to me. It's scary sometimes."

My mother knows well what I am talking about. She was there the day her mother died in Ireland. We were all there.

10

Stand by Me—Ben E. King

In the hours before Granny Nora died, I had been awake the length of the night, listening to the wind. It thrashed against the house and rattled the foundation. The roof felt as though it would lift. I'd never heard wind speak to me like that. It whistled and howled and cried like a woman. The blankets covered my ears to muffle the maddening cries. I imagined myself as Dorothy, with cows flying by the window. But I wasn't in Kansas. I was in Donegal, restlessly stirring in the middle of an autumn night as my granny lay across the lane on her farm with a nurse by her bedside.

Only a few short weeks prior, I had attended a cousin's wedding in the southern part of the country. Kneeling at Granny's feet just before I headed down to Cork, I gently placed my head in her lap as she offered me advice on my latest boyfriend. Granny was a romantic, and I knew she longed to see me find my dance partner. I blushed when she called him my lover. It sounded so bohemian. I don't think she meant it in a sexual way. She saw him as the man I loved. Therefore, he was my love, with an *r* at the end.

From the time I was a child, Granny had always walked me to the door to say farewell. She would crush me with those arms she used for picking potatoes and milking cows and then wave to me as I ducked into the rental car with my mother, father, and brother. My grandfather Pat stood with holy water, dousing the car, before we drove away and up the dirt lane covered in gravel. My mother's tears ran down her cheeks halfway to Dublin Airport. We repeated this ritual each summer.

But this time, Granny said farewell from her armchair. She sat in front of the fireplace with only the sounds of the clock and her labored breathing. She casually mentioned a pain. Her organs weren't behaving properly. I knelt there and rattled on about rubbish while she listened in silent suffering. Up until recently, this ball of energy had been dancing with Skippy, who'd bark in tune with her song. Her bicycle rarely collected dust. She was eighty-four, with her sights set on the hundred. I had attended four weddings within a period of two months back and forth between New York and Ireland. Little did I know there would be a funeral at the end of all that celebrating.

In the hours before Granny Nora died, every bed in the house was full of family from America and the neighboring counties. There were even a few air mattresses laid out on the living room floor. We had all arrived with short notice—a phone call, a plane ride, a quiet but long drive through country roads leading to the farm where I had just spent the summer. I hadn't expected to be back again so soon.

My mother gave me a look of warning before I entered the bedroom in the rear of Granny's house. I rarely saw my grandmother resting. She had already slipped into some sort of coma by the time I boarded my flight in New York. She was laid in the room I used to claim before my mother built her house across the lane.

I held my breath as I opened the door.

There she was, lying on the bed with her eyes closed. My female cousins were piled on the opposite bed, staring at her motionless frame. She was like a young bird that had fallen out of its nest, helpless and beyond repair.

We all eventually went to bed, but I couldn't sleep through the night with the wind and my memories and the knowledge that I would soon lose the only granny I'd ever known.

The wind ceased its howling. I couldn't tell if the morning had arrived yet. Not one crack of light outlined the frame of the window. My cousin Ellen snored in the twin bed beside mine. Suddenly, my bedroom door burst open.

"She's going!" My aunt Josephine urgently called into the darkness of my mother's house. She opened each bedroom door with the announcement. I leaped from the bed and struggled to find my shoes in the blackened, frigid room. I threw a fleece sweatshirt over my pajamas, and Ellen and I raced down the hall, out the front door, and across the road as an early morning drizzle assaulted our faces. My mother was already ahead of us in my granny's house.

I entered the dimly lit bedroom and found my father, uncles, aunts, and cousins standing in a circle around Granny's body. They were reciting the holy rosary, rushing one Hail Mary after the next as if to squeeze them in before her spirit left the room. I didn't join in. The prayers felt false on my tongue, like a script that didn't suit my character.

"She's gone," the nurse said midprayer, her tone emotionless.

I couldn't look at her body or anyone in the room, so I stared at my damp shoes and listened to my mother weeping.

"Go over to your mother, and put your arm around her," Ellen said.

I did it mechanically, as I didn't like being told what to do in that situation. I didn't know what to do. I just wanted to escape from the room and the tears and the pain. I wanted it to be next week or next month. I wanted the healing process to already be over. But the rawness of the reality had just begun. It was only seven o'clock in the morning.

Then everyone went into action mode. Someone left the room to call the priest. Someone went to the store to buy bread, butter, ham, cheese, and scones, plus tea, sugar, milk, and biscuits. The furniture had to be moved out of the bedrooms to make room for the onslaught of mourners. The Gardaí (police) had to be notified. Phone calls had to be made to family members who weren't present. The house had to be cleaned from top to bottom. My mother left the room and made her way to the bathroom in the hall to scrub the toilet in Granny's house, so my aunt Noreen took her shower across the road in my mother's house.

They don't hold wakes in funeral parlors in the rural areas of Ireland, as we do in New York. The wake is held in the house. The visitors would be there within a few hours—and not just a few dozen. Hundreds of them would come to give their condolences. It would be a forty-eight-hour ordeal. The Gardaí would have to control the traffic arriving on the narrow country lanes to the farm. Cars would soon be lining up and causing a traffic jam on lanes reserved for cows and tractors. Someone called the local radio station to inform reporters who announced the daily obituaries across the country. People would hear the news on the wireless and drive three hours from as far as Dublin. They might not have even known my grandmother. Maybe they had gone to school with one of my aunts or knew one of her neighbors. It was a matter of duty, loyalty, and community.

I couldn't handle the controlled crisis because I didn't know what my duty was. Emotionally exhausted and jet-lagged, I retreated outside to the cold mist and back into my mother's house to selfishly crawl under the covers of my bed. My head ached from crying and lying awake listening to the wind the night before. I just wanted to escape from the dozens of relations filling the house. The long hallway carried their voices from the kitchen down to my bedroom in the one-story house. I couldn't avoid them.

Suddenly, the door swung open, and my aunt Noreen entered the room, searching for Ellen's hair dryer. She saw me lying there, but that didn't stop her from calling to her daughter to ask her where she'd put the damn thing. She couldn't find it and stormed out of the room, slamming the door behind her. I pulled the covers up to my ears and tried to sink deeper into my pillow.

The door opened again. This time, it was Ellen. She rummaged through the wooden wardrobe and lifted unlaundered clothes off the floor.

"I found it!" she called into the hall as she closed the door behind her. This time, I lifted the covers up over my head.

A few moments later, the door opened again. It was Aunt Josephine, searching for a mirror to brush her hair. When she'd finished grooming and closed the door behind her, I thought to myself, *The next person who opens that bloody door is going to hear it from me. Can't they see I'm trying to rest here? Why don't they all just leave me alone?*

I heard the door open again. That was it! I couldn't take it anymore. I listened as the person came to the foot of the bed, and then I bolted upright to confront whichever cousin or aunt had decided to disturb me yet again. I didn't see anyone, but I knew I was not alone in that room. Perhaps the intruder was looking for her shoes. I leaned over the right side of the bed to look down at the floor and saw nothing.

Then my heart stopped.

I held my breath as the imprint of a form sitting down took its shape on top of the wool blankets. The weight of the mattress shifted. Within an instant, before my brain could translate what my eyes were seeing, a dead weight forced me back onto the pillow. My hands were up at my shoulders like those of a suspect under arrest. I was paralyzed. I couldn't breathe, crushed under the weight of this invisible force. I waited, frightened out of my mind. My eyes scanned the ceiling above me. Then a voice whispered into my left ear. It was a soft, angelic female voice. I strained to hear what the voice said, but the words were muffled as blood rushed to my ears.

I must speak, I told myself. *I must say something.*

But I lost the ability to use my voice as well as my ears and my arms. I opened my mouth, and no sound came out. I needed to ask her if she was there. I needed to know what she'd just said to me.

A high-pitched, trembling whisper finally escaped from my throat, and I managed to call out to the empty room. "Granny?"

Immediately, the invisible force released me from its grasp, and I leaped from the bed like a spring; threw open the door; and raced down the long hallway, outside the house, and across the road, where I found my mother still scrubbing the toilet in Granny's house.

"Mom!" I gasped as I closed the bathroom door and tried to catch my breath.

She looked alarmed, as I no doubt had the face of a madwoman. Crying, with spells of hyperventilation, I tried to explain my encounter using pantomime.

"I was lying in bed. Someone came in. No one was there. Wham! I couldn't move. She whispered something. I called out, 'Granny?' and—*whoosh*—she was gone!"

My mother dropped the toilet brush and covered her mouth with one hand and her heart with the other. She then wrapped her arms around me and put her head on my shoulder as tears streamed down her face.

"She always loved that room," she sobbed.

It was an odd response. How does one respond to a ghost story anyway, especially of one's own mother? But it was true; Granny had loved my bedroom.

My mother and I stood sobbing in the bathroom, holding each other, until she asked, "Did you tell your father?"

I went back to Mom's house across the lane and found my dad in the kitchen with my uncle Manus, scrambling some eggs. After motioning to him with a nod of my head, I led my father to the back bedroom. His eyes were moist because he could read my face and knew I had something important to share. I was a little more composed in my second revelation.

"Granny's spirit came to me in this room," I said. His face contorted, and he let out a gasp as he looked at me through raw eyes. His reaction brought fresh tears to my face, but I tried to keep my voice steady to share the extraordinary occurrence. I was still in a state of shock and wonderment.

"She spoke to me. I don't know what she said. I was too frightened and confused. The blood rushed to my ears and deafened me. She crushed me the way she used to hug me when she said goodbye—you know, like when you can't breathe."

He nodded as I kept speaking.

"It happened so fast. I tried to say something, but when the word reached my lips, she was gone."

I've only seen my father weep twice in my life. The first time was when his uncle Father Peter, a Jesuit priest from Roscommon, died out in Spokane, Washington, where he preached for the latter part of his life, and the second was when his father, Padraic, died in New York.

He embraced me with great force as he wept out loud. "You're so lucky. I've never experienced that."

I laughed to release some of the intensity of the moment as I stepped back and wiped my sleeve against my wet cheek. My parents' reactions were reassuring. They didn't doubt me at all. In fact, my dad was jealous!

"I don't ever want to experience that again. I don't even know if I can sleep here tonight." I looked at my unmade bed.

He wiped his face with a handkerchief he'd retrieved from his pocket. "You should tell the priest when he comes to the wake tonight."

The piercing sound of a kettle on the boil broke the silence as mourners sat around the perimeter of the sitting room beside the pantry, filling every chair and stool they could find near the fireplace. Female cousins I had never met before or met only once or twice over the years passed out homemade ham, cheese, and tomato sandwich wedges on buttered white bread. Other cousins brought teacups and saucers on trays around the room and down through the halls to the back bedrooms. Still others were in charge of collecting the empty cups and saucers and returning them to the pantry to wash for the next group of thirsty mourners. It was an assembly line of smiles and well-wishes.

"Would you like a drop, Conan?"

"Would you care for a biscuit, Méabh?"

"Milk? Och, sure it's no bother a'tall, Enda. Be back in a jiffy so I will."

A line stretched from outside the house, where the Gardaí stood directing traffic, and down the long hallway into the back bedroom, where the coffin was perched on a stand. Chairs lined the walls, filled with friends and relations who fingered their rosary beads. In some pockets of the house, people appeared to be at a party as they greeted each other with warm handshakes and winks or nods of the head. Other corners brought on fresh tears as newcomers embraced for the first time in years.

When the priest arrived, I introduced myself as Nora's granddaughter from America.

"Can I speak to you for a moment, Father?"

I led him into an empty bedroom, the one she had died in eleven hours earlier. As I closed the door behind him, nerves took over me, and I became a schoolgirl about to make my first confession. *Bless me, Father, for I have sinned. It's been decades since my last confession.*

"Something happened to me this morning after my grandmother died."

He listened patiently.

"My father suggested I share it with you."

He waited for me to reveal my thoughts when I was ready.

"Her spirit returned to me within an hour of her passing. She physically moved me as I lay in my bed, and she spoke to me, but I couldn't hear what she said."

The priest pulled on the short hairs of his black beard sprinkled with patches of gray and rocked back on his left heel as he looked down at the floor. "Tara," he said as if in reflection at the pulpit, "in times of great stress, I find that some people tend to imagine things that they wish to be true."

Imagine? I thought to myself. *Imagine?*

"I'm sure you loved your grandmother a great deal, and this mighty love may make you think that something has happened or want something to have happened, when in fact, it hasn't happened a'tall."

I stared at him.

There I was, revealing the most spiritual and sacred event that could happen in one's life, a visitation by the spirit of a loved one, a supernatural awakening to the fact that there is indeed life after death and that your spirit lives on and can communicate with those you left behind, and this man of the cloth was trying to convince me that it had not happened. Had he been in the room with me? Had he felt the crushing weight of her embrace, seen the blankets move, or heard the ghostly whisper in his ear? He had no faith in my story because it was just a story to him, told by a silly girl who was too emotional over the death of her granny to grasp reality.

Well then, Father, that must explain why I don't believe some of those silly stories in the Bible. I wasn't there either. I didn't see Judas kiss Jesus in the Garden of Gethsemane, so why should I believe that it happened? I wasn't in Lourdes, France, with young Bernadette when the Virgin Mother appeared to her and put her in a state of holy ecstasy. No wonder I go to the cinema on Christmas morning rather than to Mass. All the best films of the year are released on that day anyway.

The priest put his hand on my shoulder, smiled at me with consolation in the creases of his mouth, and then left me alone in the room so he could lead the family in prayer.

I was speechless.

Whom was he going to pray to? Whom were any of them praying to if they wouldn't believe my story? All the angels and saints? Weren't the saints the spirits of regular people who'd done great deeds or experienced heavenly visitors too? I hadn't been to church in ages, and I had my doubts about things, but that didn't stop me from praying. I always believed someone was listening. God, my guardian angel, the Universe—someone or something. There had to be something, right?

Then again, if someone had told me a relation had visited him or her from beyond the grave, I would have been skeptical and questioned the person's sanity too. That was when I decided I wouldn't share my story with anyone else besides my parents. People would just think I was crazy. Maybe I was crazy. I began to doubt myself. *Did it really happen? Why did she only come to me? Why didn't she reveal herself to my mother, my aunts, or any of my other cousins? What made me so special to get the bejesus scared out of me?*

Part 2: Metamorphosis

11

Stairway to Heaven—Led Zeppelin

I'm in a hotel. A Bible is sitting on the bedside table. I open the cover of the Bible and find a number of large bills. *The money must have been placed there for a reason*, I think to myself. It means something. Suddenly, the wall of the hotel room evaporates, and I step outside to a lush garden. It is night. I walk through the thick brush and see a sign: Garden of Gethsemane.

Well, that's helpful, I think. Then I find Jesus. He is waiting for someone. I didn't know we had an appointment. I want to ask him about the money, but I awaken before I get my answer.

I immediately sit up in bed and reach for a book. It's not a Bible filled with cash. It's my dictionary of dreams, given to me as a gift by my friend Joanne, who always finds my dreams entertaining and full of mystery. She says she never has dreams as vivid as mine, or rather, she can't remember them.

I flip through the book and search for mentions of Jesus but find nothing. As I search for other key words, I wonder again about the money in the Bible. My mind goes to the idea of prostitution because the money was left on the bedside table. But why inside the Bible? And why didn't I ask Jesus questions when I had the opportunity? The first words I was about to utter to the most recognized and holy person in all of world history were "Who left the money in the Bible back at the hotel?"

I wonder if, had my alarm clock not woken me, I would have proceeded to utilize that encounter, as I have done in an elevator when I have come face-to-face with the president of a company. I also wonder what the equivalent of the elevator pitch would have been back in the early days of Jerusalem.

I finally find the appropriate key word: *Christ*. I see three explanations of dreams one might have about this man who lived two thousand years ago. As I read the third example, an audible gasp escapes my throat: "If he is in the garden of Gethsemane, sorrowing adversity will fill your soul; great longings for change and absent objects of love will be felt."

Jakers.

What if I die before I get to do everything I've always wanted to do? This is the question I have on my mind as I head into the office. That taxi really shook me. It felt like a wild bull I had no control over, and as an inexperienced matador, I let it barrel into me. I read once that bullfighters feel most alive when they are facing the bull in the ring and living within inches of death. After yesterday's experience, I have a better understanding of what that means.

I turn on my computer when I arrive at the office and open an email reminding me about an art gallery I am supposed to visit today. As I begin to research the artist whose work I will be viewing later this afternoon, out of habit, I open a new link and type the word *Chevrolet*.

I start looking again at car-rental fees and other options because I'd really like to take this symbolic journey across America in a Chevy, just as my father's mother did back in 1957. My mood is wistful as I think about the granny I never knew. Many questions enter my mind. I knew Granny Nora my whole life, but there was much I didn't know about her until I asked, and she was delighted to share her story with me. I'm sure there are things my father and his sisters don't even know about their mother, who was taken by cancer a few short years after their memorable summer on the road. She seemed like a woman who lived life fully within inches of death. I begin to type questions on a blank screen:

What year was she born?

How old was she when she came to America?

Did she have any siblings?

Whom did she live with, and what did she do work-wise?

What was the immigration process like?

Did her ship come through Ellis Island?

What did she think about America?

Was she homesick?

When did she meet Padraic, my grandfather?

What did she like about him besides his Chevy?

What was she like as a mother?

What were her favorite things—food, music, games, sayings?

What did her handwriting look like?

What did her voice sound like?

Did she sing herself happy?

What was her favorite color?

Was she religious?

Did she ever speak of Ireland?

When did she get her driver's license?

When did she get sick?

Did she have to go through chemo?

Did she lose her red hair?

Who took care of her?

What other dreams did she have besides driving across country?

Is her spirit ever with me, like Granny Nora's, when I am anxious or lonely?

I compose an email to my father and his two sisters, Cathleen and Peggy, inserting the questions, all but the last one. I have a feeling I will get three different answers due to perspective and the individual relationships they had with their mother.

It is time to make my way downtown to a gallery to meet the artist who contacted me last week requesting a meeting. He'd like his artwork considered in some way at my organization. I haven't done enough research on him to know what to expect, but he's from Spain, and I used to live there, so I know we'll have something to talk about.

My mind is still composing questions about Granny Catherine as I enter the gallery and recognize the attractive artist I saw this morning on his website standing beside an ice sculpture that looks like the wings of an angel. He is wearing a warm, inviting smile as he speaks with a small group enlightened by his art-making process.

"I basically use ice as my medium because it is impermanent. Water symbolizes human emotion. The form of the sculpture represents the form that humans take when trapped in the physical body, but when the ice melts, just as when the body dies, we are left with nothing but the soul, which is immortal. These wings represent Archangel Michael, whom I saw during my near-death experience. He is the one who protects me now and always." The artist winks at me as I approach his group, but he continues to speak in an accent that I detect is from Barcelona.

I find myself breathing easier while listening to him, and I'm mystified by the details on the glistening angel wings, which are beginning to drip. I glance down at the brochure I picked up at the gallery entrance and admire his handsome photograph featuring a closely trimmed beard and chocolate-colored eyes.

When the attentive group thanks him and steps away, I introduce myself.

"Alberto? I'm Tara O'Grady." I extend my hand, but he surprises me and leans in for an embrace and a kiss on both cheeks.

"So delighted that you made your way here." He beams. "But please call me Toto. That is what my friends in America call me."

"Like the dog from *The Wizard of Oz*?" I ask.

"No, like the rock band from the 1980s." He laughs, showing his brilliant white teeth.

"I just overheard you say you had a near-death experience. I sort of did too—yesterday, in fact. I was hit by a taxi."

"*Ay dios mio*, are you all right?" He looks genuinely concerned, even though we've only just met.

"Yes, I'm fine, but the experience did not inspire anything like this." I look at his sculpture again. "This is gorgeous!"

"Gracias," he says as he gently touches my arm.

Toto, like his art, radiates a sense of serenity and passion. Perhaps it is his touch or something in his chocolate eyes, which hint at the answer to every question I've ever had but was afraid to ask. I suddenly feel the need to share more with him.

"I believe my granny saved me. She died a number of years ago, and I feel that she's my guardian angel sometimes." I wait for his reaction.

"Tara, *mi abuela* communicates with me on a daily basis, and she died many, many years ago. I think we need to have lunch. I have a story for you if you have time."

"I always have time for stories—and lunch," I reply, delighted that we have something else in common besides Spain.

We make our way to an outdoor café and sit under an umbrella because Toto wants to protect my "very pale skin." Today is the summer solstice, the longest day of the year. Ancient civilizations lit bonfires on this night, when the earth and sun meet as in marriage on the horizon, hence the reason we traditionally have weddings in June.

"Long story short, as they say in the movies," Toto says to begin the telling of his incredible ordeal, "I was driving in the south of France on holiday. I was not familiar with the region, and the country roads can be confusing. I looked down at my phone for directions and was not aware that a tractor had pulled out of a dirt lane, so when I looked up, I tried to avoid hitting the farmer, and instead, I hit a tree. At least this is what the doctors told me. I woke up days later in the hospital. But when I hit the tree, I remember rising above my body and seeing the white rental car, the tree, and the farmer running over from his tractor. I felt no pain; in fact, I felt wonderful. I saw and felt what I've only read about in books or seen in movies—the brilliant white light, the waves of peaceful tranquility and bliss overwhelming my spirit, the feeling of love, and the awareness of truth."

I am entranced while listening to his story.

"While my body was recovering in the hospital due to the serious head injury, my spirit was spending time with Archangel Michael. He was sent to protect me. He let me know it would all be okay but that I had to return to fulfill my soul's purpose. After I woke up and was released from the hospital, I spent a few months recovering at home in Barcelona. During this time, I often thought about the experience I had after the accident. That feeling of pure bliss was so strong I sometimes wish to return to it and escape the negative energies we create on earth with our wars, our technological distractions, and our willingness to choose destruction and hatred over creation and love. If only we knew how good the love felt, we would choose love." He beams as he speaks these words, and I get goose bumps despite the warm summer air.

"So then when did you begin to create ice sculptures, or why?" I ask as I finish my sandwich.

"I took a trip to Quebec City when I recovered. I had never been there. I just felt this intense desire to go—and during winter, which is incredible because I am a man who loves to sit on the beach in Barcelona in my bikini! Do you know how cold it is in Canada in winter?"

I laugh, nodding.

"That's where I met Gabriel." Toto touches his heart with one hand and touches my forearm with his other hand. "He was wearing these enormous white wings at the winter carnival. I couldn't take my eyes off him. It was love at first sight. We now live between our two cities. We spend the winter in Spain and the summer in Canada. But the carnival is where I discovered the art of sculpting ice. Watching the artists chisel the ice to create something so magical yet temporary made me think of how I felt altered, how I've accepted the inevitability of change, and how I now view my life as a precious gift. The way the ice glistened under the cold sun, it reminded me of the light I saw during my NDE."

"NDE?" I ask, confused.

"Near-death experience," he says nonchalantly.

Even something as extraordinary as seeing the light after death is abbreviated with an acronym. I suppose time *is* too precious to spell out all the words.

After our intense chat about his NDE, we move on to dessert, and Toto asks if I am married or in a relationship. I mention something about how difficult it is to date in New York and my theory about the distractions we encounter on a daily basis that keep us from making real connections with others.

"Have you made your official request to the Universe?" he asks as he spoons his coffee-flavored gelato.

"You mean like ordering from a catalog?"

Toto nods as I continue with a tone of uncertainty.

"I've spoken out loud about it."

"Tara," he says, shaking his head, "you need to write it down. Actually envision the partner you want, and imagine him standing beside you."

I look at him and think about his comment "If only we knew how good the love felt, we'd choose love."

After our inspiring lunch, I return to my office and write a letter addressed to the Universe—an old-fashioned letter with pen and paper, spelling out all the words. I even place it carefully in an envelope. In addition to the love note, I decide to celebrate the summer solstice after work by walking along the water at sunset in my favorite park in Queens. I want to meditate to the sounds of the seagulls.

The afternoon crawls until I take the subway home to my tiny apartment next to the Boulevard of Death, where I jump into my small Toyota and race to the park on the water's edge. It's an oasis on the outskirts of the city, with a walking path that leads to a fort on more than fifty acres containing abandoned buildings built during the Civil War. Sailboats and kayaks on the Long Island Sound pass by dormant cannons without notice, unaware of the torpedo school that existed on the peninsula in the 1870s. Cyclists, runners, dog walkers, and baby strollers pass me as I walk deep into the fort to escape onlookers until I find an empty bench facing the water. Soon a raccoon spies me from a nearby bush. We have a staring contest until he disappears into the shrubs.

At last, I am alone with my thoughts. My eyes make their way to the sky, and I watch the clouds take shape. A soft wind plays with my hair and speaks through the leaves on a nearby tree. I think about my job, the road trip, and the granny I never met. I think about Toto's words, his story, his NDE, the light, and the love.

Make your official request to the Universe.

I speak softly to the air and ask the Universe directly for what I want most.

"Please send me someone to love," I whisper to the wind, and I wait.

There are many things I want, including a cost-effective solution to how to take this cross-country road trip. But that's not what I want most. I want to find my dance partner, my right shoe, my Monday morning escort to work. *Where is he, Granny?*

I sit and wait until the sun sets, straining to hear with my left ear a message carried by the wind. But no signs reveal themselves to me, and even that damn raccoon has not returned. As the light fades, I rise from my bench and decide to visit my parents. They have a fire pit in their backyard that they sometimes light on cooler evenings when the family gathers in their garden. As an additional ceremonial boost to my superstitious activities, I decide I must light a bonfire on the night of the summer solstice, for old time's sake.

What is it about fire that connects us to the ancient spirit dwelling in each of us? It mesmerizes as its flames dance in the dark, licking the air with hot tongues of orange, snapping us into a trance. It provides a comforting heat, a temporary light in the night, and a source of survival. I gaze into the embers under the stars, surrounded by my mother's geraniums in the backyard of my parents' quiet Queens neighborhood.

"Your granny Catherine cooked over an open fire on the road trip." My father's voice enters the yard as he feeds the fire with more wood.

"Really?" I look up at him. His face is golden from the flames and his memories.

"I would catch fish in a river, and then we'd light a fire and eat out there in the wilderness. Morning was the best. She'd fry up some eggs and bacon that we'd bought at a grocery store the day before. For some reason, it tasted better out in the fresh air. She actually brought her pots and pans but realized it took ages to boil water. We mostly used the frying pan."

"Didn't you go to restaurants?"

"Occasionally. We had our first milkshake and burger at a roadside diner. But we were camping out. I slept in a tent with your aunt Peg, and my mom slept in the car."

"What about Aunt Cathleen?"

"She didn't come with us that summer. She was still in nursing school."

"You didn't sleep in motels?"

"No, we were on a budget. And it was more fun to sleep under the stars. I remember one night seeing Native Americans on horseback in the Black Hills. It was quite an adventure."

"How old were you and Aunt Peg?"

"I was sixteen, so Peg would have been fourteen."

A mosquito flies menacingly close to my ear before I swat it away. "I can't imagine camping with critters all about. When did you bathe?" I scratch my arm, now irritatingly aware of the insects.

"We would stop into a motel every third night or so but mostly washed in a river if we had the chance. It was primal. Nothing like it." He releases a bittersweet sigh into the night air.

I imagine my grandmother sleeping in the backseat of her Bel Air and think about how I lock my car doors out of habit the second I sit inside my Toyota.

"It wouldn't be safe to sleep in a car today. A woman couldn't do that." I look at my father, who shrugs.

Suddenly, my mother's voice calls from the kitchen through the sliding screen door.

"Women didn't leave their husbands either and drive across country in the fifties for an extended holiday." She is pouring milk into her tea before she joins us in the garden.

"She was adventurous." Dad folds his arms across his chest, shifting in his chair.

Mom opens the sliding screen door and closes it quickly to keep the mosquitoes out of the house, all the while steadying her cup of tea in her other hand, and then settles into her chair by the fire. "Never mind adventure. She was smart. I couldn't get away with not having a dinner on the table every night of the week for this man." She nods toward my father. "I'm surprised Pat O'Grady let her go."

"How long were you on the road?" I ask my father.

"Seven weeks," Dad says.

"Seven weeks without a bloody dinner? Ha!" Mom rolls her eyes. "I could see me trying to pull that with you, and here it being 2011."

Dad ignores her comments and continues with his story. "She didn't call home until we found a pay phone in Yellowstone. Your grandfather was furious. Worried sick. Thought we had gotten lost or attacked by bears or something."

"He wasn't worried." Mom looks at me and winks. "He was hungry."

When I finally get home to my apartment, smelling of smoke from the ceremonial fire, I turn on my computer before bed, a habit I must break, and find a number of messages from a variety of men.

One is an email from a guy I met at a networking event this past month named Conor Gallagher. Another is a message from a guy I also met recently, Manus O'Donnell. Their last names are the maiden names of my grandmothers, Nora Gallagher, my Donegal granny, and Catherine O'Donnell, the road-trip granny. Then I read a Facebook message from an Australian boyfriend I dated a few years ago. He writes from South Africa, where he is enjoying a football match and watching the sunset overlooking hippopotamuses. He wonders what I am doing in celebration of the summer solstice. I am not about to tell him I watched the sunset overlooking raccoons in a park in Queens and lit a ceremonial fire to communicate via smoke signals with the Universe.

Finally, the last message makes me question the sense of humor of the Universe. It is from a stranger. He saw me performing online. He sent me a friend request on Facebook from Europe and wrote that his friend sent him a YouTube video of me performing in New York. Apparently, while viewing the video online, he "fell in love" with me. I understand that love at first site is a powerful emotion, as Toto experienced when he met Gabriel, but when it comes with computerized emoticons, I am a little wary. I investigate the stranger's profile and learn that he is already in a relationship and, in his own words, "obsessed with money." A photo portrays him in a white suit and black shirt reminiscent of *Saturday Night Fever* starring John Travolta. I click to ignore his friend request after reading his message: "Tell me—do you have a man in your life?"

Do I have a man in my life? It's the question on everyone's mind, especially mine. Does Tara have a man in her life? No! That's why I made my official request to the Universe, as Toto instructed. I wrote a letter. I lit a fire. I spoke to the night wind as raccoons eavesdropped. And I seem to have received a response. I've never been contacted by so many men at once.

As I lie down in bed, I think about the raccoon who glared at me during my ritual. I've been reading about the presence of animals in our lives because I tend to dream about lions, tigers, and bears (oh my), and my dream book reveals that each animal spirit has a symbolic meaning. For example, when I saw the rooster in the snowstorm, it made me think of Granny Nora. I learned that a rooster spirit symbolizes courage, confidence, and chasing away evil spirits. I definitely had more courage to drive in the snow when I saw it before me. Raccoons, on the other hand, are clever and find everything they need through constant exploration. They wear a mask, which is a symbol of transformation.

Is that what the Universe is trying to tell me? That the presence of the raccoon tonight is a sign I am about to explore and transform into someone new, into who I am destined to be? That both my grandmothers are watching over me, not just my Donegal granny? That old flames are still lit? That I should be careful with the information I put out into the world via the internet or ceremonial fire?

I know one thing: the Universe is faster than my internet connection.

12

Over the Rainbow—Judy Garland

Toto emails me and invites me to his going-away party, as he is returning to Canada since his publicity tour is over. He decides to host a picnic at dusk under the canopy of trees between the opera house and the reflecting pool outside Lincoln Center. He brings strawberry shortcakes, cheesecakes, chocolate mousse cakes, fresh fruit, and sparkling cider. We will no doubt get high on sugar. I arrive early after my workday to help him gather chairs in a circle, and I find myself in an argument with a miserable man who says we can't horde all the chairs, as it is a public park. I ask him if he is using any of the chairs, and he says no, so I tell him to mind his own business then and keep his nastiness to himself. Toto is disturbed by the level of rudeness in the city that never sleeps. Perhaps it's the lack of sleep that makes everyone so grouchy.

"Are there any straight single men coming tonight?" I ask Toto.

"No, but did you perform your cosmic ordering, as I suggested?"

"I did." I sigh, not knowing what to make of it all.

"Well, keep yourself open. What you need will come to you. Remember, if it's for you, it won't pass you."

His words echo in my ears.

As his friends gather, I listen to them chat about reiki, meditation, and aromatherapy over our sweet cakes and cider. One man takes a small maroon satchel from his backpack and produces a number of little bottles with a variety of essential oils.

"Have you ever smelled frankincense?" he asks as he turns his attention to me.

"Is that what the three wise men brought to Jesus?" I respond, looking at his wedding ring.

"Yes. It's from a tree in Yemen that can grow out of solid rock." He shows me the writing on the bottle.

"I thought frankincense was a treasure, like gold." A June breeze blows a strand of hair over my eye as I try to read the bottle.

"It was considered just as valuable. It has been traded for five thousand years along the Arabian Peninsula. They slash the bark on the Boswellia tree until the resin bleeds. They call the resin tears and use it as incense in the temples in Jerusalem."

"And how do you use it?" I brush my hair away from my face.

"During aromatherapy sessions. Wanna try?"

"Sure!" I am always up for a new experience.

"The aroma is said to represent life. Different faiths use it to anoint newborns and individuals moving into a new phase in their spiritual lives," he says as he unscrews the tiny bottle cap. "Are you sure you are ready for this?"

"Yes, why?"

"It's powerful stuff. It slows and deepens your breathing and awakens a higher consciousness. It's like getting high."

"I've never been high. I don't drink or take drugs." I stare at the bottle in his hand, eager to inhale its contents.

"Well then, this is the closest you will ever get to being high."

He leans into me and places the small bottle under my nose, directing me to breathe deeply. "Take another breath." He breathes with me, demonstrating how to get the most of the ancient aroma into my being.

The effect is immediate and intoxicating. I feel light-headed and elated.

"Hit me again!" I demand as he laughs.

"Okay, just one more swig, and you're done."

The little bottles are just as expensive as illegal-drug addictions, but I'd be willing to pay for that biblical high again. Wise men indeed.

I'm feeling giddy, when I notice a middle-aged woman with long black hair, sun-kissed skin, and a radiant smile sitting alone. I move over beside her.

She tells me her name is Christine, and we chat for a while about life, travel, and the world at large until she makes me an offer.

"Would you like to have a creativity session?" Christine asks as she hands me her card. "Just call my number, or email to set up a time. You can come to my office."

I don't know what she is talking about, but in my state, I am up for anything. It sounds interesting. Everything sounds interesting, from the leaves gently blowing in the breeze to the laughter in the distance of couples hovering over the reflecting pool and sitting by the fountain spouting water orchestrated by an invisible symphony. Lincoln Center at night is one of the most romantic spots in the city.

"How's tomorrow?" I ask eagerly.

After an uneventful day at work, I arrive in the lobby of a building on the Upper West Side, and a doorman asks me to wait until I am summoned. I feel as if I am in the waiting room of a doctor's office, but this is the lobby of an apartment building. I'm confused. Christine finally emerges from behind a door and invites me into a space that is an apartment transformed into a professional office. Still uncertain of her business, I walk around her office, admiring the artwork on the walls and the baby grand piano in the corner of the room.

"Are you a musician?" I ask, pointing at the piano.

"I used to perform quite a bit. I even sang backup for Barry Manilow." She laughs. She has an easygoing way about her that makes me feel relaxed.

She offers me a seat on her red couch and pulls up a desk chair directly in front of me.

"What exactly do you do for a living now?" I ask her, looking at the framed diplomas on the wall.

"I'm a psychologist." She smiles.

Oh Jaysus, I think to myself. *A head-shrinker? Why the hell did she invite me to therapy?* I feel as if I've been hoodwinked.

"I thought we were going to have a creativity session." I look at her suspiciously.

"We are. I got the sense when I was speaking with you that you had a great energy and creative spirit. I thought you'd benefit from a session with me," she says, still smiling. "I sometimes work with soldiers who have returned from Afghanistan and Iraq. I help them reenter civilian life. But I also work with artists. I help them open up their creativity. Everything exists in a state of possibility and change. This includes your feelings and ideas of the world and of yourself. You mentioned that you sense a disconnection between what you want and what happens to you."

"Yeah, I guess." I am still trying to figure out why I'm in her office.

"There is a joy that comes from fulfilling your heart's desire. It's effortless for an artist. Michelangelo explained that he didn't create David out of stone but, rather, revealed him in the stone. The reason he was able to see David in the stone is because David was already inside of him."

"So what does this have to do with me?" I eye her warily, wondering if I have to eventually pay for this knowledge.

"I wrote a book that helps people discover their full potential." She hands me a book with the title *Ignite the Genius Within*. "I sensed something in you that needs to be revealed."

"We just talked about dual citizenship." I try to recall my conversation with the shrink, who apparently has fully explored her abilities to psychoanalyze people. I'm getting a little spooked. What does she know about me that I don't know about myself?

"Let's try something and see what happens." She takes headphones out of a drawer. "I chose the sound of waves crashing on the shore. I have all sorts of sounds, but I think the ocean would be good for you to start this session." She places the headphones on my ears, and I hear the sound of waves undulating from one ear to the other like a tennis match at the beach.

"Can you still hear me?" she asks, and I nod. "Okay, I'm going to talk to you, and you can close your eyes and listen to my voice. Just let your thoughts go wherever my voice takes you. You will be leaping through time and space. Just let your mind wander."

I close my eyes, and at first, the sound of the ocean going back and forth between my ears makes me dizzy, but I try to concentrate on her voice to prevent seasickness. She guides me to relax my body and think about each muscle because she can see that I am tense. I didn't expect a therapy session, so of course I am tense. But Toto advised me to be open to whatever comes, so here I am, on the couch of a psychologist, listening to the ocean going in and out of my ears like the waves on the Donegal shore, with the seagulls flying overhead and the wind blowing the tall grass along narrow roads that lead down country lanes. I am on the dirt lane next to my grandparents' cottage. I am a toddler, one or maybe two years old—old enough to walk. I am near the metal gate at the back of the house, the one that leads to the fields where the cattle chew the grass and where Granddad picks potatoes row after row and lights bonfires on the summer solstice. I hear Granny Nora in her kitchen. She is baking scones and singing to herself. She is close, just around the corner, just inside the door. I could go inside to see her again, to hold her, tell her I love her, and ask what she said to me on the day she died, but I don't want to go inside the house. It hurts too much. The pain of her loss—it's as if she just passed away. Even though she is so close, I can't reach her. I stay outside in the body of a toddler, kicking stones, staying close to the ground. My throat feels tight, and I feel as if I am about to cry. I hear myself say this out loud, and Dr. Christine tells me to think of the pain in another part of my body so the pain in my throat is relieved. I put the pain in my foot, in my big toe, as far away from my heart as possible, and suddenly, I am a young woman wearing a spaghetti-strapped dress, sitting alone in a rowboat with my bare feet dangling over the side and my big toe playfully skimming the painfully cold water. The boat is drifting out of a dark cove and into the open ocean, but I can't see beyond the darkness, as fog is rolling in. I'm not afraid despite the darkness and drifting into the unknown. I'm curious to know what is beyond the fog, but Dr. Christine tells me to bring my awareness back to the room, and I open my eyes.

"You did very well." She beams, taking the headphones from me.

"I was in Ireland. I was a child, and I saw my grandmother inside the window." I feel as if I have just awakened from a nap.

"Yes, you were telling me everything you saw," she says, still smiling a comforting smile.

"Did you hypnotize me?"

"The sound has that effect on the brain, putting the listener in a waking dream state. It enables people to bring thoughts and feelings to the surface."

"How long was I under your spell?" I ask.

"About an hour."

"An hour? It felt like five minutes!" I can't believe my mind traveled so far. Time and space were meaningless, like in a dream. "So how will this help me?" I ask as I look at Dr. Christine with new appreciation.

"You have the power to create. Everyone does. Creativity is an expression of your own power to turn every moment of your life into a work of art. If you want to write, you can use this process to mine your memories. If you want to sing, sculpt, paint, or dance—whatever you want to do—you can use this method to find the artist within. Your mind is already experiencing your heart's desires. This is an instrument to help you use your own awareness to see that everything you want to have, you already do; everywhere you want to go, you're already there; and everything you want to be, you already are. There is no distance between you and happiness, only in your ability to see it."

I need to digest these ideas. It is all too much to handle for one evening. I still don't know why she gave me the session for free with no strings attached. She didn't even try to sell me the book. She gave me a copy at no cost, along with the soundtrack of the ocean. Has living in New York hardened me so much that I can't even trust someone who wishes to share something with me? I wonder if she knows how valuable her gifts are.

Your worth is determined by your service to others.

Those words from my recent dream come to me again. Dr. Christine is definitely someone whose worth is determined by her service to others. All those soldiers who've come to her office with wounded spirits must have shed some of the tears of their resin from the bark of their experiences, surviving in places that miraculously permit growth from unforgiving, barren terrains. She, after a session with them, most likely is left with a contact high from the aroma of war. I can't imagine listening to the stories she has heard. But I am eager to imagine the life I want to create for myself.

13

See the USA in Your Chevrolet—Dinah Shore

I've made it to Friday. In only one more week, I will officially be unemployed—or retired, as I've been referring to my current state, teasing my parents, who have always worried about my future.

"Another day, another thirty-two cents," I mumble to myself as I plop down at my desk across from my cardigan-wearing coworker.

I pick up the map of America as I wait for my computer to awaken. Dr. Christine's words enter my mind: *Everything you want to have, you already do; everywhere you want to go, you're already there; and everything you want to be, you already are. There is no distance between you and happiness, only in your ability to see it.* She reminds me of Glinda the Good Witch from *The Wizard of Oz*, and I laugh to myself as I look down at my favorite pair of red high heels.

I have no desire to open work emails, so I again type the word *Chevrolet* into a search engine. I scan some links I haven't looked at before. Then, suddenly, something catches my eye. *Chevrolet's hundredth anniversary!*

"No way! Seriously? When?" I say out loud, astonished by my find, and for some reason, my coworker responds.

"When what?" he asks, not turning from his desk.

Sure, now he's listening.

"Nothing," I respond as I continue to scan the page, but I can't find anything more.

Then I type the name of the iconic car company into *Wikipedia*, and the site reveals that Chevrolet did indeed begin in

1911—November, to be exact. *Jackpot!* What is it with that month, the eleventh month of the year? Everything meaningful or significant to my family seems to have occurred during that month. My mom came to America on a boat on November 11, I had my first kiss on November 11, and I fulfilled Granny Nora's last wish to visit her house in London on November 11.

I pick up my phone and call my father.

"Hey, Chicky!" He has many pet names for me despite my age.

"Hey, listen. When was your mother born? I mean, what is her birthday?" I wait as I hear him thinking, but I have an idea of what the answer is going to be.

"She was born in"—he's trying to calculate the years—"1908."

"And the month?" I ask eagerly.

"November. November 19, 1908."

"I knew it!"

"Why?"

"I just figured out a way to do the road trip!"

"How?"

"Chevy is going to pay for it."

"How are you going to make that happen?"

"Just you wait, 'Enry 'Iggens!" I sing in my best Eliza Doolittle impression, and I hang up to the sound of my dad laughing.

"Are you singing *My Fair Lady*?" My coworker turns around on his swivel chair, smiling at me sheepishly.

"You really have selective hearing, don't you?" I roll my eyes at him as he shrugs.

Now the what-ifs are flooding my brain. What if I contact Chevrolet and get them to pay for this symbolic road trip? What if I tell them I'm honoring their anniversary by taking the exact route my Irish immigrant grandmother took? But how will I get their attention? *Come on, Tara. You're creative. Think.*

What if I get my amazingly talented brother, Tom, to assist me in making a video? We could use the old photographs from the 1957 road trip. I could interview Chevy owners and have them gush about their vintage cars. I could inform the CEOs at General Motors that I've been laid off from my job, lots of Americans are suffering right now, my granny came to this country because of the American dream, and life is all about fulfilling dreams. I'm sure the owner of Chevrolet had a dream. We all have dreams. I brainstorm my ideas on a Post-it note and see the distance between me and happiness growing smaller.

Saturday evening is when the Northeastern Queens Hot Rod Association assembles their vintage cars on summer weekends in the local parking lot in front of my parents' supermarket. I was not aware of this assembly until recently, as I don't make a habit of hanging out in supermarket parking lots on Saturday nights, but due to my extensive research online of all things Chevrolet, I have come to learn that as with any obsession, there are fan clubs. This is a fan club I would definitely like to join, but I don't own a classic car. That is a key requirement for membership.

On Saturday, I make my way to the parking lot in Queens, where I approach a group of men standing proudly beside their cars.

"My Irish grandmother drove a '57 Chevy Bel Air from New York to Washington state back in the summer of 1957, and I'm interested in taking the same journey, so I'm making a video for Chevrolet to see if they will sponsor my road trip. Would any of you gents be interested in telling me more about your cars for my camera?" I swallow hard, intimidated by what they are wearing: shirts known to Queens' residents as wife-beater tank tops. Many of them also wear gold crucifixes around their necks and large pinkie rings.

"Sure, talk to my brother." One of the tough guys walks me over to a cigar smoker. "Hey, Vinny, this young lady wishes to speak with you. She works for Chevy."

"No, I don't work for Chevy," I say, correcting him. "I'm just making a video about Chevy owners."

His brother looks at me through narrowed eyes, as if I'm with the IRS, the FBI, or the Jehovah's Witnesses.

"I just want to know the year and make of the car and perhaps why you own a Chevy." I wait for his approval.

"Awright, how you want me to stawt?" His Queens accent is stronger than his brother's.

"Just state your name, and tell me about your car," I say, lifting my camera and focusing him in the frame.

"My name is Vinny. This is my 1970 Chevelle. There's nothin' like a Chevy. It's been the greatest caw since the fawties. Fifty-seven is still the nicest caw Chevy eva made. Doesn't compare to Fawds. Doesn't compare to Chryslas. We owned all Chevys as a kid. They make a nice caw." He finishes and takes another puff of his cigar.

"Thanks." I shake his hand.

"So you work for Chevy?"

"No, I just want to drive across country in a Chevy," I say.

"Oh, like the song." Vinny begins to sing, holding up his razzmatazz jazz hands: "See the USA in ye Chevrolet! America is askin' you to call." He sings the advertisement jingle from 1953, which has been in my head for weeks now.

"Listen to this bozo." His brother raises the back of his hand to Vinny, who flinches.

"What do you drive?" the brother asks.

"A Toyota," I mumble, looking at the ground.

The men groan.

"Don't eva say that out loud. You could get hurt in this neighborhood," Vinny teases.

"May I sit in your car?" I ask another man nearby who has been listening.

"Yeah, sure, knock yerself out, kid. Just don't get yer prints on it." He opens the door of his 1957 Corvette, and I carefully slip down into the driver's seat like Cinderella into her glass slipper.

Why did we ever stop making such beautiful automobiles? Not

many cars today inspire this much imagination. I place my hand on the steering wheel and look back at the Italian American brothers.

"You look like you belong in that caw," Vinny says.

"Don't give her any ideas." The owner jabs him playfully in the ribs.

"Could one of you take my photo, please?" I ask, and Vinny reaches for my camera.

As I smile at the lens, the early evening sun creates a halo around his silhouette, and I get the feeling that somehow, everything is about to change. I do feel as if I belong in this car, in this moment, as if it were meant to happen, and it's only just the beginning.

I race to my brother's house in Long Island so he can record me before the sun sets, which would mean we'd lose the light for the exterior shots I have envisioned. He has a quaint all-American front porch with a white railing and a wooden swing that my dad built for him and his wife to rock their children to sleep. I have my script prepared, and he has his tripod in place. As soon as I pull up and park, he sets me up on his porch and points at me when the camera begins rolling.

"Hi. My name is Tara O'Grady, and I come from a Chevy family."

I beam at the camera and explain the history of my grandparents' relationship, including how my Irish grandmother married my Irish grandfather for his 1934 Chevy; got cold feet on the steps of the church but listened to her convincing girlfriends, who reminded her that he owned a car; and eventually bought a 1957 Bel Air and packed it up that summer with her pots and pans, her two teenage children, and her sense of adventure.

"I never met my father's mother. She died before I was born. So in honor of her spirit and the one hundredth anniversary of Chevrolet, I'd like to follow in her footsteps across the country and just take that great American road trip."

The light is fading fast. The sun has gone down behind a house across the street, but we manage to capture the last few lines as dusk approaches.

"I just got laid off from my job. Times are tough. A lot of Americans are suffering right now. But I have hope, and I think America does too. I want to find out if the American dream still exists. I want to ask people what their dreams are. I want to see the USA in a Chevrolet and follow in my grandmother's path. I want to search for America's spirit and document it all. Know anyone who'd like to lend a gal a ride?"

We move inside the house to my brother's basement, where he has his office and computer. I've never seen anyone work as quickly as he does when it comes to editing and manipulating images. He is a genius with technology. He copies the footage of the Northeastern Queens Hot Rod Association and a photograph of me in the 1957 Corvette. Then he uploads the establishing shots we have just recorded. I hand him the old photographs that were in our father's shoebox, including the one of Granny Catherine sitting on the 1934 Chevy on her first date with our granddad, the one of the whole family sitting inside the new Bel Air before she drove it across country, and even a few from Yellowstone and Montana. Tom scans them into his computer.

"What about music?" he asks.

"Use my song 'I Want to Go to There.'"

He uploads an original song I cowrote in Nashville for my second album. In the lyrics, I sing about all the places I've always wanted to go to. My voice is now filling the room, and my brother visually orchestrates the images to match the sounds of the music on his computer. I leave him to his masterpiece and go home, knowing that a fully edited professional video will appear in my inbox by morning. He's that good. He always beat me at video games when we were growing up. Atari's joystick did not bring as much joy to me as it did to my brother, who resembles Tom Hanks with his dark curls and boyish charm.

As suspected, I wake up to the edited video in my inbox. It's brilliant. The old photos, the family history, the interviews with

Chevy owners, the music, and my mission statement—it all makes me cry. I watch it over and over.

"Tom," I tell my brother, "you are amazing. I love it! I couldn't have done this without you."

"What's next?"

"I email the video to General Motors headquarters in Detroit and wait."

14

On the Road Again—Willie Nelson

The last week in the office drags. It is rather uneventful despite a few lunches with friends I've made over the years. On my final day, I take down my Audrey Hepburn postcards, images of the Irish landscape, and lists and Post-it notes of things I want to do and places I want to visit. I pack a box with my map of America, coffee mugs, unused tea bags, and other personal items while listening to coworkers cry and say farewell to each other. I have no desire to participate in the sob fest. I am looking forward to leaving this space. I find it strange that I feel no emotion, not even resentment. I have been frustrated in this place, so my only feeling is one of relief as I walk to the subway, ride home on the International Express, enter my tiny apartment next to the Boulevard of Death, wash the city from my face, make myself dinner, and go to sleep.

My alarm clock awakens me in the morning. I must have set it out of habit. The song playing on the station is one I recognize but never have listened closely to before. I hear a lyric about getting a new job on the unemployment line, and it forces me to sit up straight in my bed to focus on the words. The singer asks if God is testing him, because now that he's lost his job, times are tough.

"That was the Script with their song 'For the First Time,'" the radio personality says across the airwaves.

The first tear falls, and within seconds, I am swimming in a bed of tears, sobbing uncontrollably, mourning the loss of my job and my existence as I knew it. I worked in that office, in that space, for five long years. The rowboat is now drifting out into the ocean through the fog, and I have no anchor or compass to guide me.

What do I do now? I ask myself through the sobbing. *What happened to Confident Tara? Can't-Wait-to-Get-Out-of-Here Tara? I've-Got-a-Backup-Plan Tara? Where is she?* She is drowning in her bed of self-pity and loss.

After a cup of coffee and a lot of cold water splashed onto my face to reduce the redness, I feel a little better. I'm actually thankful this release has arrived. I was beginning to wonder why I felt so unnaturally elated for the past two weeks while my coworkers, some of whom I called friends, were devastated and why I showed them no support or empathy. Perhaps it was a defense mechanism. At least now I know I am human. I haven't cried like this since Granny Nora died.

I bring a second cup of coffee to my desk, where I turn on my computer and open my email—another habit. I'm used to turning my computer on the moment I arrive at work to check my email, but now I get to do it without a shower, and I can sit in my pajamas all day. I don't ever have to leave the apartment again—or bathe, for that matter. I can have everything delivered: food, books, and whatever else I need. This could be dangerous. I need to start looking for a job.

I begin to delete junk mail, until I look more closely at an email address I don't recognize. The subject line reads, "Chevy Cross-Country Road Trip." My heart rate quickens. My eyes race over the words on the screen as I see that the message is from General Motors. They loved the video! They think my voice is amazing! They want to secure a vehicle for me to make my trip across America! I am offered three choices: a convertible Camaro, an Equinox, or a Duramax-equipped Silverado truck.

I reread the email three times just to make sure I understand the offer. I jump up from my desk and do a happy dance around my tiny apartment, screaming until I am out of breath. I reach for my phone because I want to call my parents, my brother, and Lauren, but I don't know who to call first. I decide to call my parents.

"Hello?" my mom answers.

"Put me on speaker!" I shout into the phone.

"What? Are you okay?" She is concerned by my excited tone.

"Is Dad there? Put me on speaker. I have to tell you something!"

"Okay, he's here. What's going on?"

"Chevy responded! They are giving me a car for the road trip!" I am breathless.

"Oh my holy God." My mother sounds dumbfounded.

"What did they say?" My dad is ecstatic.

"They are offering me an Equinox, a Camaro, or a Silverado pickup truck." I already have a website open to examine the vehicles. "I want all three! I can't believe this!"

"When are you going to go?" my dad asks. I can hear the emotion in his voice. This was his mother's journey, and I am about to relive it.

"I don't know. I have to plan. I have to pack. I have to ask Lauren. I'm too excited. I can't concentrate. Let me call you back."

My brother's reaction is the same. He is genuinely excited for me. I let him know GM really liked his video. I can hear him smiling on the phone.

I finally call my copilot.

"Louise, this is Thelma. Guess what?" I can't contain the excitement in my voice.

"Shut up! Did they? Are we?" Lauren knows what I am about to tell her.

"We are going on a road trip!"

Part 3: Migration

15

Sentimental Journey—Doris Day

I'll never forget my first love; took my breath away. I gasped the first time I saw my love drive by. What a body. Talk about photogenic. I had an "I'd go anywhere with you" look in my eyes upon first sight, and I would have gone anywhere. I'd have hit the road and run away from home with no forwarding address. That's the kind of love it was. To this day, when I see an old photo, I still sigh breathlessly to myself. Stylish. Fast. Electric. I couldn't wait to go for that first ride, if you know what I mean. Rebellious personality. I liked rebels. They were adventurous and spontaneous. They'd take you anywhere you wanted to go. And I wanted to go far—really far. I wanted to go to the moon and back, with Elvis crooning on the radio, the wind blowing through my hair, and everyone staring at me from the sidewalk, wondering, *Who's that girl?* Why, that's Tara O'Grady, cruising the boulevard with her first love.

My first love was not a fifteen-year-old boy. It was a fifty-four-year-old car. No man could have given me that much pleasure.

The historic Chevrolet dealership in Queens where my grandparents purchased all their cars over the decades hosts a going-away party on a bright September afternoon the day before I leave for my road trip. Their PR man invited local media, but not one newspaper or network has come to the event. A gal chasing her granny's spirit across the USA in a Chevrolet is not newsworthy, I suppose. Perhaps we should have staged a shooting or run over a pedestrian with one of the new Camaros on the Boulevard of Death.

I don't need a cameraman; I have my dad. He is documenting the event like a *National Geographic* photographer.

"Move a little closer to the cake," Dad says. I lean over the red, white, and blue icing, which reads, "Good luck, Tara," as Mom stands next to the two-foot-long salami hero.

The PR man has displayed a large map of the United States, with the route I am going to take outlined in fluorescent pink marker. The mechanics of the dealership pop confetti with at least three dozen employees who have gathered for the occasion in their matching sky-blue shirts and dark navy pants. Some of the men hide their eyes under the brims of Yankees caps. Others give me shy but encouraging smiles as I glance down at their name tags—Jose, Carlos, Raj.

"We stand here today because a young lady named Tara O'Grady came into our dealership and wove this wild tale about a road trip in an intoxicating video," the PR man says, beginning his speech as Dad hands his camera to an employee so he can stand beside me in the shot. "She spoke of the American dream and about her grandmother, who drove from this very location all the way to Seattle and back. Her grandparents purchased cars at this very dealership over fifty years ago," he says proudly. "She is using the East Hills Chevrolet as the beginning and end of her symbolic cross-country journey, and we want to thank her family for being a part of our family."

Dad looks as if he's going to cry.

The owner of the dealership surprises me with gift cards to pay for hotels, since he's learned I only have a few couches secured, in Cincinnati, Chicago, and Seattle.

Now Mom looks as if she is going to cry.

The dealership also surprises me with a few dedicated customers who own 1957 Chevy Bel Airs. A bright yellow classic car and a racy black model are parked on either side of the 2011 Equinox the dealership is loaning to me.

I run my hand down the lines of each model like John Travolta in *Grease*, caressing their wing tips. The beauties look ready to fly like lightning—greased lightning.

With permission from the owner, I open the door of the yellow Bel Air parked outside the dealership and finally climb inside a model of the car Granny Catherine drove across country. Fingering the interior, from the wheel to the seats to the dashboard, I examine the speedometer and gasoline gauge. I imagine Granny sitting in the car and looking in the rearview mirror. I glance at the backseat. It doesn't look comfortable for sleeping. I wonder if she wore pajamas. I know from photographs she mostly wore dresses. We don't put on our Sunday best anymore these days, even on Sundays, but every day is like a Sunday in a Bel Air.

The next morning, I rise with the sun and greet the first day of driving with nerves. A checklist runs through my head as I force-feed myself breakfast. I'm afraid to drink too many fluids because I don't want to have to keep stopping, but I'm also worried I'll get dehydrated. As I pull out of the driveway at seven o'clock, it's as if I'm swimming away from the edge of the pool and into the deep end for the first time.

Queens grows smaller in my rearview mirror, and the Bronx fades away. As I leave New York City in my wake, crossing over the George Washington Bridge, I become blinded by emotions.

I'm about to drive across America!

I think of my grandmother and how my grandfather assumed she would turn back on that very bridge and go home, giving up on her dream to cross the country and see the wild American west.

She was a typical 1950s housewife in some ways. She wore dresses every day; made fruit-salad parfaits, Jell-O molds, and blueberry pies; and kept a tidy house. My aunts informed me their mother loved America because it was modern. She left Ireland in 1927 because, like her future daughter-in-law (my mother), she found no opportunities in her homeland. Jobs were scarce, but America held promise.

Granny Catherine initially worked in a hospital in London as a teenager, but she had an uncle in Massachusetts who wanted to sponsor her. Her sister Anna was already working in a house in

Worcester. My dad's mother took the same sea-sickening passage from Cork that my mother took but landed in Boston rather than the Big Apple. She returned to Kilmacthomas, Waterford, by boat a number of times over the years to visit her parents, Denis and Bridget O'Donnell, but America dazzled her, so she had no desire to ever live in Ireland again.

Catherine and her older sister Anna weren't afraid of hard work. They were domestics who lived in the same house as a nanny and a cook. My granny was apparently wonderful with children. The children she cared for played with little Teddy Kennedy, and when his brother eventually ran for office, Granny voted for the first time as an American citizen because she knew the family and wanted to see an Irish Catholic in the White House.

She had only just gotten her license a few short years before the road trip. My grandfather refused to teach her how to drive; he didn't think it was necessary. She could walk to the shop to buy groceries, as all the other housewives did, he told her as her children raced behind her. They couldn't keep up with her pace, as their legs were shorter than her temper.

When Granddad left New York Easter week to visit his family back in Roscommon, she asked his Irish coworkers to teach her how to drive her husband's 1950 dark green Chevy. Her new sense of freedom was documented in a photograph as she waved from the driver's seat during a lesson.

Seeing the enthusiasm on her face, you'd never think she recently had lost a newborn. I didn't know I had another aunt. She died on the day of her birth due to complications and the doctor's incompetence. She was named Monica Lewis O'Grady after Granny's favorite film star and jazz singer. Monica Lewis was on the first episode of *The Ed Sullivan Show*. She was also the voice of the Chiquita banana advertisement. I didn't know Granny Catherine liked jazz as much as I do.

When my grandfather returned from his holiday in Ireland, his wife declared she was going to drive across country—as soon as she learned how to turn around. She drove her children to Mass that Easter Sunday but didn't know how to make a U-turn. Soon enough, her skills improved, and there was no stopping her. She became impulsive and didn't think twice about jumping into the car to go somewhere—anywhere. It was the adventure of the journey that excited her, not the destination, and the independence that came with having a license to drive. She wanted to feel the wind blowing through her red hair and tear up the open road as far as it would take her.

After I get off the George Washington Bridge, I take a wrong exit and end up on a highway that my father advised me to avoid. New Jersey always confuses me. I've already made a mistake, and I'm not even twenty miles from home. I suddenly become doubtful. *Can I really do this? How can I drive across the entire country?*

I have to drive the first day alone—eleven long hours in the car. I have never driven for longer than five hours to visit Aunt Peg in Lake Placid up in the Adirondack Mountains. My copilot, Lauren, is waiting for me in Cincinnati, where she has been visiting her mother. The plan is to pick her up there, as she is my designated photographer for the journey. For symbolic reasons, it'll also feel comforting to have a redhead beside me, but right now, my nerves are beginning to take over, and my navigator keeps repeating, "Recalculating," in her irritatingly robotic tone, so I turn on the radio.

"The Occupy Wall Street protestors are growing in number since they began their sleep-in at Zuccotti Park in Lower Manhattan on Saturday."

I'd rather hear music as I occupy this vehicle for the next three weeks. I search for another station. A song comes on the satellite radio, one I performed with my jazz band at a send-off party I hosted in Manhattan last week: "Let's Get away from It All." It makes me smile and relax a little. I hum along with the melody. Granny Nora always sang herself happy.

The following song is Bing Crosby's version of "Red Sails in the Sunset." Bing attended Gonzaga University in Spokane, Washington, where my grand-uncle Father Peter taught. Granny

Catherine was going west to visit Father Peter, her favorite brother-in-law, in Spokane. Interestingly, the song is about a sailboat in Ireland.

What a coincidence, I think.

Next, "On a Slow Boat to China" comes on the radio, another song I performed with my band at the send-off party. All three songs mention travel by boat and have some connection to me. I think of the rowboat drifting out of the foggy cove into the dark ocean—the vision I had under Dr. Christine's spell.

This is more than a coincidence. This is Granny Catherine letting me know she is with me. I pull off the road to get a cup of coffee at a McDonald's and call Dad to tell him about the three songs.

"You're still in Jersey?" he asks, not fully appreciating the significance of the satellite song selections. "Get back in the car. You have six thousand miles to cover!"

As I enter Pennsylvania, I wonder how Granny drove without air-conditioning, cruise control, airbags, or OnStar. I have my laptop, video camera, smartphone, and digital camera, as well as an additional portable navigator; a safety kit; hand wipes; Windex and paper towels; chargers for all my electronic devices; extra batteries; a digital voice recorder; Chevy posters and stickers that Chevrolet sent me to hand out along the road; my music CDs to give away; a cooler containing apples, oranges, grapes, water, ice, and sandwiches; a bag of chips, chocolate bars, granola bars, trail mix, and herbal tea; an ice scraper for the windows; a pillow; an umbrella; Woolite; plastic cups; utensils; earplugs; makeup; a hair dryer; toiletries; one pair of red high heels, which I call my Dorothy shoes, as they remind me there's no place like home; flip-flops; boots; bathing suits; and wool sweaters (the seasons are changing, so I have to cover both summer and fall).

Many of my items are invading the backseat as well as the passenger seat. I have no idea how Lauren, let alone all of her stuff, will fit in the vehicle tomorrow. She often carries numerous bags on the subway, so I assume she'll have double the amount for the road trip. I've definitely brought too much. I'm sure Granny's artifacts were significantly less complicated and packed neatly in the trunk of the Bel Air. She wore the same few dresses every day, hand-washed her unmentionables, and stopped to buy food when she got hungry.

I must learn how to simplify.

I've also brought two books with me: my dictionary of dream interpretations and Mark Nepo's *The Book of Awakening: Having the Life You Want by Being Present to the Life You Have*. In one essay, titled "Grief," he writes about where the redwood trees talk with God and how he carries his grandmother behind his left eye, where the spirit sees. He explains, "Grief is yet another song the heart must sing to open the gate of all there is." I think that's just about the best sentence ever written by anyone anywhere.

It's time to stop for lunch. The exits have been much farther apart since I left New Jersey, so I keep my eyes peeled. The highway cuts through rolling green hills containing horses, cattle, red barns, haystacks, and fog-covered cornfields. If it weren't for the eighteen-wheelers dominating the lanes, I would assume I am in Ireland.

The next exit is for Donegal, Pennsylvania. I can't believe it. I never knew there was more than one Donegal. In the weeks leading up to the road trip, my mind was always on my father's mother, the granny I never met, but here is a sign reminding me of Donegal and the grandparents who crushed me with their love on their farm where they milked their cows, picked their potatoes, and sold their eggs. As I pull off the highway and into a rest stop, a butterfly dances around my car. It remains while I eat my lunch outside at a picnic table. I call my mother to tell her I am in Donegal. My father sits beside her, examining a map he purchased in the morning at his corner store. He wants to follow me with his finger.

"You are off the course I initially planned for you," he says into the receiver as Mom pulls the phone away from him.

"Tell him I was meant to be here, Mom," I say as I get back into the car to continue to Ohio, which is where Granny Catherine also stopped on her first night.

When I return to the highway, I notice another butterfly flit across my window. I've brought Windex and paper towels because I read that a lot of bugs sacrifice their lives on the windshield during long road trips. I have never killed a butterfly, and I pray one won't land on my window at sixty-five miles an hour. Another one zags past the car.

What are they doing out here on the highway?

Then a shower of butterflies storm my path one after the next, crossing the highway directly over my car. Dozens and dozens of determined butterflies zoom by, coloring the sky with their elegant brilliance. I call my parents back and put them on speakerphone.

"The migration!" I shout.

"What?" My mother is confused. "Are you okay?" Her voice is full of concern.

"I'm in the middle of the butterfly migration!" I exclaim in astonishment. "They are flying south for the winter!"

It is the end of September. They are migrating to Mexico from North America. They have until November 1 to get to their destination—a day Mexicans celebrate as Dia de los Muertos, the Day of the Dead. As that young girl at the Bronx Zoo mentioned, Mexicans believe the butterflies are the reincarnated souls of their ancestors returning home.

All the ancestors fly above me as I migrate west to chase my granny's spirit. But I never needed to chase her spirit. She was always with me, behind my left eye, where the spirit sees.

It's nice to meet you, Granny Catherine.

16

I've Got the World on a String—Cab Calloway

I finally enter Cincinnati under a blackened downpour with my thoughts lingering on butterflies. This is the farthest I've ever driven in one day, and with the way my back feels, I'm not sure how I'll make it through the next three weeks.

After I rest for the night in Lauren's mother's apartment, my redheaded copilot reorganizes my belongings in the back of the Equinox under an early morning drizzle. As I suspected, she has a lot of stuff, and when it's combined with my stuff, we can barely see out the back window. We keep the brownies her mom baked for us close to the front seat. They won't last the day.

When we finally get the car organized, my enthusiasm returns. "Are you ready, Louise?" I look over at my copilot as she buckles her seat belt.

"I'm ready, Thelma. Away we go!" She waves to her mother, who snaps shots of us as we pull out of her apartment complex.

I push the OnStar button on the rearview mirror, and a heavenly voice enters the Equinox.

"Welcome to OnStar. This is Wendy. How may I direct you?"

"Good morning, Wendy. This is Thelma and Louise, and we're on a cross-country road trip," I tell the helpful stranger.

"That sounds like fun. What is your first stop?"

"Moraine, Ohio, please."

"I'll download those directions for you now. Anything else I can assist you with today, Thelma and Louise?"

Lauren and I look at each other and laugh.

"No, thank you, Wendy!" we shout in unison.

A robotic voice replaces Wendy and informs us we should start by going north on Raglan Road. I smile at my copilot. It's good to finally have a passenger in the car to chat with. I didn't realize I could have had Wendy or any of her OnStar colleagues chatting to me across the foggy cornfields of Pennsylvania. We never have to be alone. Someone is always there to guide us.

We head to the DMAX manufacturing plant near Dayton to take a tour. This is not a stop that was on my grandmother's original journey, but we were invited by the people who make the Duramax diesel engines installed in Silverado pickup trucks like the one we'll be picking up in Chicago in a few days. They heard about my symbolic Chevy road trip because the video I made with my brother went across the globe and back. Apparently, my friend Liz in Hong Kong saw it on Facebook and forwarded it to her friend who works for GM; he forwarded it to his friend Ted, who works for DMAX in Ohio; he forwarded it to some head honcho in Detroit; and voilà!

Ted, the controller at the plant, has been emailing me all summer to prepare us for our experience. It is nice to finally meet the friendly face behind the emails. When he greets us at security, we have to promise the gentleman behind the desk not to take any pictures inside, where the engines are built. I've never been inside a manufacturing plant before. It is an exciting privilege.

Ted hands us NASCAR goggles as he leads us behind the curtain to meet the great Wizard of Ohio. There we find Mitch, a no-nonsense engineer who is the assistant manager of manufacturing. Mitch leads us on an hour-long tour of the plant, where he has designed every inch of the layout. It is massive. It feels like an airplane hangar.

Lauren and I receive curious looks from the five hundred employees on the assembly line. We are wearing matching gray

Chevrolet T-shirts that read, "American Beauty," in bright pink letters—compliments of Chevy headquarters—and matching Audrey Hepburn scarves tied around our necks. We stand out.

Mitch explains how the engines are built from start to finish. With each question I ask, he realizes I am genuinely interested in the development of his company's product, so he goes into more depth describing each step of the mechanical process. I take notes as he speaks. He shows us the chunk of metal that comes over from Japan on a ship, as General Motors has a joint venture with Isuzu. In one section of the plant, there are Japanese employees who spend three to four months working in America. (Maybe that's why I had a dream about Tokyo last night in Lauren's mother's apartment in Cincinnati.) The chunk of metal eventually transforms into a fully functioning engine that they test in a soundproof room on the opposite end of the plant. In one eight-hour shift, 336 engines are built by this team of five hundred employees assisted by melodious robots.

Mitch and Ted warn us to stay on the walking path and look both ways when we cross from one lane to another as the moving robots transport materials to different stations. The robots play classical music to alert employees of their locations so no one gets run over like pedestrians on my Boulevard of Death back in Queens. Making motors to the sounds of Mozart. That is truly inspiring.

We are introduced to a number of hardworking employees, including the outgoing Tamecka, who waves to us from a distance. She and Mitch share a jovial exchange despite his seniority. As they speak, I notice Tamecka is wearing a T-shirt with a butterfly on it. That makes me smile. Mitch steps closer to me when he sees me scribbling in my little notebook.

"What are you writing?" he asks, concerned I am stealing company secrets.

I show him the page, and he reads it out loud to Ted.

"Tamecka—butterfly T-shirt." He looks bewildered as Ted laughs, adjusting his prescription eyeglasses.

"She has a thing for butterflies," Lauren says as I put the notebook away, not wanting to cause any more concern for our friendly and informative tour guides.

Lauren and I are impressed with how many women are working on each team, even one who looks eight months pregnant. *You go, girls!* Granny Catherine believed women should work and have their own income. Her dream was to become a licensed nurse. She planned on attending nursing school in Washington, DC, when she first came to this country, but she ended up getting sidetracked and moved from Worchester to New York to be with her favorite sibling, Jack. That's where she met my grandfather, who didn't want her to work or drive. He was old school. But she convinced her daughters to pursue nursing and teaching careers. Nothing was going to stop them from getting advanced degrees—she made sure of that.

I am also impressed by the teamwork in the plant. One of my goals on this road trip is to see what America is up to work-wise. I encounter many disgruntled commuters on the subway each day returning from long hours in the city. It appears no one is happy with his or her day job. But these Ohio residents, these guys and gals on the assembly line, are smiling and whistling while they work. They greet us with gusto. They teach us about crankshafts, harmonic balancers, and air tests. We have a number of in-depth conversations about how they believe in the quality of their work and expect nothing less than perfection from their colleagues. If an engine doesn't pass inspection at the end of the day, it goes back for tests until it is 100 percent perfect and ready to be placed in the number-one selling truck in America. I am inspired by their drive and enthusiasm.

Ted and Mitch eventually lead us up to their offices, where they give us goody bags filled with snacks for the car, as well as DMAX T-shirts and little toy models of '57 Chevy Bel Airs. I name mine Belle.

"This is from our CEO." Ted hands me the sealed plastic bag filled with Life Savers, Tootsie Rolls, and M&Ms. A white label on one side of the bag has the typed words "Good luck from the DMAX team!" I can't imagine a CEO in New York preparing such a simple and personalized gift. It is heartwarming. That's when I pull out my American flag.

One week before the road trip, New York City was recognizing the tenth anniversary of September 11. I was honored to be asked to perform at a dinner for the first responders. The organizer requested songs with a respectful tone. I didn't know how I would get through the evening all the while remembering the worst day of my life. I had to prepare three hours of jazz and blues and listen to speeches that made my throat tighten up. In addition to "Danny Boy" and "The Water Is Wide," I sang "What a Wonderful World" and "Over the Rainbow." One by one, throughout the evening, responders from as far as Oklahoma City approached the stage and thanked the band for our music. They included volunteers from the Red Cross and Salvation Army, ironworkers, hard hats, FDNY, NYPD, EMS, Department of Transportation, tradesmen, and a number of civilians. The eleven-year-old daughter of a first responder sang "God Bless America" as well as Celine Dion's version of "The Prayer." Bagpipers marched into the room in their brilliant kilts and disciplined manner.

After dinner, my band asked me to sing "I've Got the World on a String." It wasn't on the set list. I hesitated at first but then thought, *Why not?* After I sang the song, I spoke to the crowd for the first time that night. I told them that every time I sing that song, I think of September 11 because I was singing it to myself the moment the second plane hit.

The room grew silent, and a woman stepped closer to the stage. "What did you just say?" she asked.

My thoughts returned to the worst day of my life.

———

I was on a bus going to work in Manhattan during rush hour. I was singing to myself, "I've Got the World on a String," because the sun was shining, and I had a new job. It was only my second day. I was alive, the seasons were about to change, and I felt as if I were *sitting on a rainbow*, just like in the lyrics of the song.

I didn't know he entered the towers that day. *What a world.*

He stole a kiss on our first date, and I adore stolen kisses because those are the ones I remember when the blue notes begin and because the men who give them are daring, and I like men who know what they want.

He always wanted to be a fireman. *What a life.*

He looked at me as no other had looked at me before, as if he wanted to save me and devour me at the same time, and my heart danced under his gaze. He smelled like the ocean, and I wanted to wade through his blond hair and dive under his sun-kissed skin. I thought he was the one, and I'd give anything to be kissed like that again, with the smell of the ocean and the sound of the seagulls.

Lucky me, can't you see... it was love.

——

I cleared my throat and carefully repeated my statement into the microphone. "I was singing 'I've Got the World on a String' the moment the second plane hit the Twin Towers." I looked down at my feet, remembering the fear, uncertainty, and pain of that day and the many days that followed. I'd give anything to be kissed like that again.

Grief is yet another song the heart must sing to open the gate of all there is.

Suddenly, the room burst into applause. A union carpenter who was also a US veteran took a photo of me and gave me a thumbs-up. I stepped off the stage to speak with him. As we got to talking, I informed him of the great American cross-country adventure I was about to begin. He then reached into his bag, took out a large folded American flag, and handed me an eight-by-ten photo of him with other responders marching from the pit at Ground Zero eight months after the attack. The two flags on each end of their banner were a part of America's labor history, he informed me, and part of a collection of patriot flags from the US Patriots Organization, whose flags were proudly flown at Ground Zero, the Pentagon, the Flight 93 site, the Statue of Liberty, and Uncle Sam's grave.

As the DMAX team poses for a photo while holding up the American flag the veteran gave me on the September 11 anniversary, Ted points to numbers handwritten on the corner in black marker. "What's this?" he asks.

"The first responder wrote, '1957,' to honor my granny's spirit, and he asked me to display the flag on the Chevrolet as I drive across country, to remind Americans about their sacrifice on and after September 11."

"Thank you for sharing that story with us. We can't imagine what that day must have been like for New Yorkers." Ted adjusts his eyeglasses as his team stands beside him, looking at their feet.

"Don't forget," Mitch says, breaking the silence after a long, respectful pause, "the Silverado only takes diesel fuel."

Lauren and I thank the team for their time and generosity. It has been an inspiring afternoon.

As we head to the parking lot to get back on track and reach the next state on Granny's route mapped out by the good people of the Automobile Association of America, we hear voices calling to us.

"Bye, Tara and Lauren!"

Employees are going home for the day and getting into their Impalas, Malibus, Blazers, and Avalanches. Every one of them owns a Chevrolet.

"Good luck seeing the USA in your Chevrolet!" They honk their car horns as they drive past us.

I look over at Lauren, who grew up in Connecticut, Indiana, and Ohio before she moved to the big, bad city.

"Is everyone this friendly outside of New York?" I ask.

She laughs as she climbs into the Equinox. "Actually, yes. Isn't it refreshing?"

"It is," I reply as I look up at the bright September sky, imagining I hear a seagull flying by.

17

My Way—Frank Sinatra

We approach Chicago, the city Carl Sandburg personified as "laughing the stormy, husky, brawling laughter of Youth."

"Come and show me another city with lifted head singing so proud to be alive and coarse and strong and cunning," he shouts in his poem, which is named after the city itself.

So far, I have driven through seven states: New York, New Jersey, Pennsylvania, West Virginia, Ohio, Indiana, and now Illinois. Once I left the congestion of New York City, with its bridges, bypasses, and red lights, it was all cornfields as far as the eye could see, along with big, beautiful windmills dancing like daisies at dusk. I'm not used to so much space. It feels unfamiliar. Donegal, Pennsylvania, felt familiar because it looked like the rolling green hills of Ireland, but America is beginning to look like one flat plain and one long highway.

As we approach Chicago, the drive is like playing leapfrog between a cornfield and the Sears Tower. Suddenly, without warning, the country turns into the city, and I feel comfortable again. I know cities. I understand them. I might not love the crowds, congestion, and chaos, but Chicago feels like a floating device as I head out into the deep end of the pool of America the Beautiful.

Lauren and I are staying on our second couch of the journey in the Windy City. We only have couches waiting for us in Cincinnati, Chicago, and Seattle and otherwise will have to book hotels day to day, depending on where we end up. I don't know how Granny slept in the car every night. Where did she go to the bathroom in the morning?

My friend Fayth meets us on Michigan Avenue, where she lives with her fiancée, Jordan, and their two little rescue dogs, Pippen and Tino. Fayth is a dancer from New York. Jordan is an actor from Kansas. They met at an arts college in North Carolina. When they moved from the Big Apple to pursue their performing passions, they sent me an open invitation to the less intimidating metropolis of Chicago. I gladly accept, as I have never been to the city, which has been referred to me as a cleaner New York. I can't really tell how clean it is, as it's already night when we arrive, but I don't see any rats yet, so that's a good sign.

Fayth takes us to her dance studio, which is across the street from her high-rise apartment building facing Grant Park and Lake Michigan.

"You own your own studio?" I ask as I wrap my arms around her tiny dancer frame. I haven't seen her in almost a year.

"Yes, my dance company practices here, and I also teach Pilates." She leads us on a tour of her equipment and office.

"You have your own dance company?" Lauren asks, just as astonished as I am by this mature twenty-five-year-old Italian American. She is a young female entrepreneur who left home to pursue her dream. I admire that. But I wonder if she is homesick.

"So what made you leave New York?" I ask, examining the spacious studio, which features mirrors on one wall and large images of her leaping, jumping, and dancing on the other.

"New York was a bit oversaturated with mind-body fitness studios, and I have always loved Chicago. It was more affordable, and I knew I could find a niche here," she responds as she organizes fitness equipment in a corner of the lime-colored studio.

"Will you dance for us?" I am eager to see her move in this space. I once saw her perform a few years ago at Lincoln Center. Her choreography that night was described as ambitious.

Fayth flips through songs on her iPod. "I find this song to be the most inspiring when I dance." She smiles as Frank Sinatra's voice fills the room.

"'My Way'? Ooh, I love that song too." Lauren wiggles like Marilyn Monroe in anticipation of the intimate performance.

We watch as Fayth glides through the room, her elegant limbs reaching with Sinatra's sentiment. Her movements intensify as Blue Eyes climbs the lyrics. She dances as if she doesn't have any regrets. She dances like a woman who has loved, laughed, and cried. To think, she has done all of this at the age of twenty-five. She obviously emerged from her cocoon way before I did. I am envious of her accomplishments and of her engagement to a handsome and equally talented young man. Perhaps dancers find their dance partners sooner. But my admiration outweighs my envy, and watching this young woman dance in her own studio makes me hopeful. I am witnessing the American dream in action.

Chicago always has beckoned the ambitious, as we learn on a historical architectural cruise of its canals with Fayth and Jordan. Our amusing guide on the tour boat informs us that this city put up the first cloud buster to create the skyscrapers of a modern metropolis. It's also the city that electrified the blues.

As we eat a late breakfast of complimentary freshly baked cookies with coffee on the tour boat, Fayth informs me that her dad once owned a 1957 Chevy Bel Air.

"I'm really envious that you are on this adventure," she says as we float under a bridge near the *Chicago Tribune* building. "I'd love to just take off and go somewhere."

She doesn't look as if she gives herself much time off from her budding business. She was in her studio late last night, and this is her first tour of her new city. She wants to take a break from her long hours in a job she created for herself, and I'd like to have a job, especially in a creative field. I'd also give anything to have a fiancée, as she does.

Why do we always want what others have? We often overlook how abundant our own lives are and forget to be grateful for our blessings. Modifying our wants decreases our suffering. We must learn to make a distinction between what we want and what we need. At this moment, I want a slice of pizza.

Lauren and I say farewell to Fayth and Jordan when our boat returns to its dock. The couple must go back to work. Jordan has to rehearse with the Timeline Theater Company because he is performing in a play later this evening called *The Pitmen Painters*, which is about miners in Northern England who took an art-appreciation class that transformed how they looked at art and their own lives. He's reserved tickets for us and says we will be meeting the cast for a bite afterward. However, Lauren and I want a bite at this moment and begin our search for a slice of pizza.

As we walk the streets of Chicago, past the *Chicago Tribune* building and the larger-than-life statue of Marilyn Monroe, whose white dress is blown up by the Windy City, exposing her matching white undies, I realize I have to make a distinction between *want* and *need* to decrease my level of suffering. We can't find one single pizza shop in the entire city, and I decide I *need* food—any type of food will do. That's when we see a sign for the number-one hot dog in Chicago.

We enter the eatery, and our hungry eyes scan the brightly lit fast food joint: a map of America is painted on one wall, and dozens of framed photographs of customers standing in front of American landmarks, such as Mount Rushmore, the Golden Gate Bridge, and Wrigley Field, are on the opposite wall. We are on the corner where Route 66, the two-thousand-mile highway that leads travelers to get their kicks, begins.

We stare at the menu above Karen, the counter girl, as she patiently waits for us to choose which kind of dog we want to order. There is a hot dog for almost every city across the country. The Chicago Dog comes with mustard, relish, onion, peppers, tomato, pickle, and celery salt. The Dallas Dog comes with chili, onion, and shredded cheddar cheese. The New York Dog comes with sauerkraut and brown mustard.

"So what will it be, ladies?" Karen waits.

"We just can't decide. We're beyond hungry," I complain, thinking of Granny Nora, who never complained. Sure, who would listen to her anyhow?

"And we can't believe the concept of your store. We're on a road trip!" Lauren says. "We're driving to Seattle."

"The owners are siblings, and they went on a road trip back in the 1990s and sampled hot dogs in every city." Karen points to a sign on the wall: Notes from the Great American Road Trip. Lauren and I look at each other.

"Another extraordinary example of putting passion to work," I say to Lauren.

"Two siblings took a road trip for fun and turned their experience into a business," she adds.

"The American dream at work," we say in unison and look at Karen behind the counter. She simply smiles and tells us to have a nice day.

As we bite into our all-American dogs—I ordered the Memphis Dog smothered in pulled pork, barbecue sauce, and coleslaw, and Lauren has the New Orleans Dog with barbecue sauce, sautéed onions, and tomatoes—we know we were destined to find this establishment. Yes, the hot dogs live up to their reviews. We don't need to try any other dog in Chicago to know these are numero uno.

Lauren and I arrive early at the Timeline Theater in Chicago's Lakeview East neighborhood, so we decide to window-shop before the performance. One little shop catches our eyes and ears because it is speaking to us. It says, "Take off your coat, and stay awhile. I'll even put the kettle on." The lighting is warm, and the smile on the girl behind the counter is even warmer.

I am drawn to a rack of vintage-looking scarves. I finger the rack until one of the scarves calls to me. It is white with tiny green polka dots and a raspberry-colored owl with a peach-colored breast under a raspberry crescent moon. The owl is a symbol of hidden intuition, and a crescent moon symbolizes a new chapter in one's life. I imagine

Granny Catherine would have worn something like this, so I bring it to the counter to make my purchase.

Lauren steps up beside me, holding a postcard. "Look!" She points at the blank map of America. The message on the card reads, "It's Not That Far, Really."

"I can stamp that for you," the shopgirl says.

"We're on a cross-country road trip," Lauren says.

"Well, that's what these are for. I can stamp where you begin and end with my heart." She pulls out a heart-shaped stamper and dabs it in a container of red ink. "Where do you want me to put the hearts?"

"New York and Seattle." I point at the tiny states outlined on the map.

"Wow, well, actually, that is pretty far," the shopgirl says as she places her heart on my postcard.

"I'm chasing my granny's spirit across America in a Chevy and searching for the American dream. Do you think it still exists?"

The shopgirl's eyes light up with enthusiasm, and she comes out from behind the counter to introduce herself properly. "Oh yes. I'm Stacy, by the way." She extends her hand. "I opened this shop using a small business loan in order to support friends who are artists. These are all their works." She points to the artwork on the walls and shelves. There are prints, paintings, sketches, crafts, jewelry, and all sorts of unique artifacts. "I make silk-screen cards myself. I believe in mom-and-pop shops and that customers appreciate knowing the creator of a product rather than purchasing something that was mass-produced. It makes for a more personal connection."

"I agree," Lauren says, placing a necklace on the counter to purchase.

As Stacy rings us up, I tell her more about my Chevy-sponsored granny quest, and she listens with her whole being.

"What you girls are doing reminds me of why I opened this shop to begin with. Sales are down, and I'm struggling to pay my bills each month, but sometimes we need to be reminded of why we're doing what we're doing. And your story makes me believe that I'm on the right path."

"As long as you are following your dreams, you are going in the right direction." I look into Stacy's eyes. *She can't be a day over twenty-seven*, I think to myself. I've never met so many twenty-something-year-olds with their own businesses.

She comes out from behind the counter again and gives me a hug.

Lauren looks at her watch. "Tara, we're going to be late for the play!"

I sit in the theater, wearing my new polka-dot owl scarf and holding the postcard with hearts stamped across two locations on the map of America. As the actors portray life in a 1930s mining town in England, putting paint to canvas for the first time in their lives, expressing themselves in reds, blues, and blacks, I think of my granny Nora, who went to England in the 1930s to marry a man for love, and I think of my granny Catherine, who was in New York at that time, marrying a man for his potential. I look down at the heart stamps in the illuminated Chicago theater and imagine what the printout of a heart monitor would look like not just as scribbled lines on a hospital's spreadsheet but in colors, shapes, and sounds from a lifetime of ups and downs.

What would Granny Nora's heart monitor have looked like, with her wedding day in London in 1939 at the start of war, having to move back to Ireland, and losing her firstborn to America?

What about Granny Catherine's, with her arriving in Boston Harbor, hesitating at the door of the church in New York, having a miscarriage, driving across America, and finding out she had cancer?

What about my heart monitor? I imagine it would be purple and zigzagged and sound like a saxophone in Central Park, with more ups than downs but enough downs to balance the ups for perspective's sake. Strong enough to manage the journey and to do it my way, like Sinatra sang, because I have the power to manifest my destiny.

18

Blue Suede Shoes—Elvis Presley

In the morning, I rise with Chicago at my feet and Lake Michigan stretching out in front of me like the unknown waters in my hypnotic state under Dr. Christine's spell. Lauren and I say farewell to Fayth, Jordan, and their entertaining and energetic little dogs, Pippen and Tino, who woke us up bright and early. It is time to pick up the Silverado in East Dundee, outside of Chicago, and move further out into the deep end.

We are supposed to meet a man named Fred. I have never met anyone named Fred. I only know of three Fred's, all fictional: Fred Flintstone, Fred from *Scooby-Doo*, and the guy Audrey Hepburn's character Holly Golightly called Fred after her brother in *Breakfast at Tiffany's*, even though George Peppard's character's name was actually Paul. Audrey called him Fred Dahling. I begin calling Chevy Fred that as well. He doesn't mind. He probably thinks we are just two silly girls out for a joy ride. He actually looks like the *Scooby-Doo* Fred and Audrey's Fred combined with his blond hair.

Fred Dahling helps us unload the Equinox and transfer all our stuff into the massive truck as I glance down to see a wedding ring on his finger.

"How long will you be on the road?" he asks as he lifts one suitcase after the next into the flatbed.

I know what he is thinking. *Yes, we did overpack. Don't throw your back out, Fred Dahling.*

"Three weeks," I respond. "Chevy only gave us three weeks. My grandmother spent seven weeks on her road trip. She wasn't limited to a rental period, even though we're not exactly renting."

Fred Dahling apologizes in advance. "Yeah, we need this puppy back for a charity event next week in Chicago."

He then gives me a brief orientation to the new vehicle. After he points out the basics of the interior, I ask if I can see the engine. "We were just at the DMAX plant where they make the diesel engines, so we'd like to see the finished product under the hood."

Fred Dahling is impressed. Perhaps we aren't two silly girls out for a joy ride after all.

I hop down from the towering height of the cab and follow him as he proceeds to lift the hood. The front of the truck rises above my chest. I have to stand on the tips of my toes to see the engine. I want Lauren to take a photograph so we can send it to the DMAX team.

"Lauren?" I call to her, but she doesn't answer. I thought she hopped out of the truck the same moment I hopped out so we could both look under the hood. "Lauren?" I call again. "Where did she go?" I look at Fred Dahling, who shrugs.

She sheepishly appears from behind the massive vehicle.

"What happened?" I look at her as she starts to laugh.

"I fell out of the truck," she says as her cheeks take on a shade of bubblegum pink.

"You what?" I can't contain my amusement and bend over, slapping my knee.

"I didn't realize how high it was, and I ended up flat on my face," she says through tears brought on by the fit of laughter.

"Are you okay?" Fred Dahling asks, concerned.

"Yeah, I'm just embarrassed," she says as we both lose control altogether. This is going to be an interesting challenge.

When Chevy initially offered me the choice of three vehicles for my journey, I tested each one at my grandparents' historic dealership with my proud father by my side.

"It's like trying on a pair of shoes," Dad told me. "It's a long haul. You have to be comfortable."

A black convertible Camaro was the highlight of the showroom, but after I sat in the driver's seat, the new car felt like a pair of uncomfortable stilettos that were too tight. I couldn't wear that for six thousand miles.

Roger, the friendly salesman, then led us outside to the lot filled with trucks and SUVs.

"There she is." He pointed to the Silverado pickup truck with the Duramax diesel engine.

"What?" I shaded the sun from my eyes as I looked at the titanic vehicle. "I'd need a ladder to get into that thing."

Roger opened the door for me, but I had trouble climbing up into the driver's seat. The monstrosity of the truck intimidated me. It was like a pair of stiletto cowboy boots on steroids. The wheel made me feel as if I were driving a bus. I had never driven anything so massive.

"I'm not sure about this one." I looked at Roger as he rested his elbows on the driver's-side door.

"Well, this is the type of vehicle you'd want going over those mountains. It's not meant for city streets."

I awkwardly slid down from the driver's seat, hanging on to the steering wheel as if it were a nautical lifesaver. Roger then led me to the final choice: the Equinox.

"Most women prefer this vehicle," he said in a tone that didn't contain the pressure of a sales pitch but felt sexist.

I stepped inside the SUV, and the seat welcomed me with a warm embrace. It was like a pair of plush bedroom slippers—a perfect fit. I felt like Goldilocks. The Camaro was too small, and the Silverado was too big, but this was just right.

As I adjusted the seat, my cell phone rang in my pocket.

"So what did you choose?" Mom's voice was always warm. The longest road trip she ever took was from her farm in Donegal to the dock in Cork.

When my mother arrived in America, she saw her father's face in every man on the sidewalks of Manhattan. Her uncle met her at the dock where her ship came into New York Harbor and passed the Statue of Liberty. She couldn't have cared less about seeing the symbol of freedom for the first time. Coming to America was more of a prison sentence to her. She never wanted to leave Ireland. But every young person who had connections in America migrated for money.

Her uncles and their wives and friends handed my seventeen-year-old mother ninety-two dollars as a welcoming gift. She immediately mailed the cash home to her father, as he'd had to sell one of his cattle to pay for her passage. He begged her in a letter not to send any more of her hard-earned cash once she got a job, so she could return to Ireland one day. However, since the boat ride was so sickening, she decided she'd only return by plane, and she couldn't afford the price of a flight for five torturous years because she always sent her money home to her parents.

In April 1998, I went to Amsterdam because the tulips were in bloom, and I wanted to see Anne Frank's house at Prinsengracht 263. I was teaching literature, and her diary was on the syllabus. I convinced my mother to join me on my annual birthday trip. She was hesitant at first because her father was dying of pancreatic cancer. Granddad had been suffering for eight long months. But I selfishly convinced her she needed a holiday because I didn't want to travel alone and assumed the trip would keep her mind off things. She obliged but called Ireland every day to check on her father's status.

Granddad died soon after we returned to New York. Mom should have flown straight from Amsterdam to Ireland. She didn't make it in time to hear his last breath. My uncle Manus sent a taxi for her to drive the three hours from Dublin Airport to the farm. Halfway through her journey, my uncle called the driver, who pulled over to the side of the road, and Mom got out and roared into an empty field until there was no sound left in her lungs.

Grief is yet another song the heart must sing to open the gate of all there is.

She called me in New York. It was six in the morning. I was getting up for work. I cried in the shower and wondered how I could face the day. But I had to return to the school because I had scheduled an afternoon field trip for my twelfth-grade film class. We were going to the American Museum of the Moving Image to see Hitchcock's *Psycho.* That was exactly how I felt, psychotic.

A student in my first-period class wrote in her journal that morning, "I saw my teacher cry today." I scribbled a line from Anne Frank's diary on the board using chalk. Anne wrote the entry on the exact day, month, and date of my birthday, Tuesday, April 11: "We Jews mustn't show our feelings, must be brave and strong, must accept all inconveniences and not grumble, must do what is within our power and trust in God."

Before my grandfather died, he was still trying to work the land on his farm. The man was in his eighties and suffering from pancreatic cancer, but he wanted to get his antique tractor to work. Granny Nora asked if she could help him, as she had always helped him on their farm.

"I can drive it, Pat, sure. How hard could it be?"

"Nora, the battery is dead. You'll not get beyond a stone's throw. Sure you don't even know how to start or stop the bloody thing. You've only ever ridden a bicycle."

"I can push you, Pat. If you hop on and get it going, I can push the tractor to get it jump-started."

"Nora, you wouldn't have the strength to push me even if I was off the tractor."

"Oh, I'd find the strength, Pat. For you, I'd find the strength."

Granny Nora had only driven a car once in her life: at Coney Island, when she came to visit America for the first time in 1962 to see her daughter get married. My mother's younger sister, Noreen, had migrated to New York when she finished school and soon found an Irish American husband in Brooklyn. Aunt Noreen and my mother took Granny to the amusement park on the boardwalk. Granny wanted to drive a bumper car but couldn't get it to do anything except spin around in circles. The ride operator kept shouting orders at her as other drivers rammed into her sides. She held an audience for ages, laughing at her incompetence. But she was certain she could do anything if she put her mind to it. She simply believed she could do it.

Mom's voice was still on the line as I sat in the Equinox at the historic Chevy dealership in Queens.

"So which car did you choose?"

"The Silverado seems a bit big, but I think I can handle it," I told her, thinking how fortunate I was to have my mother and father near me whenever I needed them.

I finally made my decision. I chose the Equinox to drive from New York to Chicago because it did indeed feel like a pair of cozy slippers, but I also chose the Silverado to drive to the mountains and beyond. Although the massive pickup truck intimidated me, I wanted to drive it for the sake of being out of my comfort zone. Besides, I didn't want to fall into the category of "most women," as Roger the salesman had put it.

If Granny Nora thought she could push a tractor and Granny Catherine got a license without her husband's permission and drove six thousand miles on her first go, I knew I could handle this.

"I think I should drive first," I say as I look at Lauren, who is still in stitches from falling out of the truck.

Fred Dahling shows us where to fill up the tank with diesel, and he tops it up for us before we drive out of the gas station and on our way to Sioux Falls, South Dakota.

"He was cute." Lauren beams, waving back to Fred Dahling, as I pull the monster truck out of the station. "He probably thinks we're idiots."

"You were the one who fell out of the truck. You're falling for the wrong guy. He had a wedding ring," I say.

"You think I didn't notice?" Lauren is single too, recently divorced. We are both looking for love. But I think I've found it. I start squealing in delight.

"What?" Lauren looks at me.

"I'm driving a big ole pickup truck!"

We briefly drive through the corner of Wisconsin, with its violets and hickory trees, and I wonder about emerald dragonflies and prairie bush clovers, which are now as endangered as the prairies of Minnesota, which were once thick with tall grasses blanketing the rich farmland of the early settlers. As we enter the Midwest, now only patches of prairie are visible, interrupted by the paved concrete, sprawling out from under the highway and into the abyss.

Then I see a sign: Welcome to South Dakota. I never relinquish the wheel that first day in the Silverado. I let Lauren play with the radio stations and search for hotels on her smartphone.

"It's getting dark, Thelma." Lauren yawns.

"I know, Louise, but I want to get to Sioux Falls tonight."

I don't like driving in the dark, as there are no lights outside the cities. Granny Catherine always stopped driving every day around four o'clock. That gave her time to shop for something to cook for dinner over the open fire and let her teenage children pitch their tent and set up camp.

Lauren's phone beeps. As she reads the text, she lets out a sigh.

"Why are boys so frustrating?" she grumbles, throwing the phone back into her purse.

"What now?" I ask, not knowing if she's referring to her ex-husband or a new interest who isn't showing enough interest.

"Ah, it doesn't even matter." She sinks back into the front seat. "They're all the same. They string you along, they can't commit, they are vague, and they don't follow through. I'm sick of it. Why don't men act like men anymore?"

"You're preaching to the choir. I haven't had a date in six months." I adjust my lights on the dark highway.

"I mean, what's wrong with them? We are attractive, intelligent, and fun, dammit!" Lauren huffs.

"It's not like it used to be when my grandparents met."

"Don't I know it?" Lauren sighs. "'Till death do us part' has become just a scripted vow." Lauren stares out the side window into the darkness with her red head leaning against the glass. Her parents divorced when she was a teenager.

"I read this book by Dick Meyer called *Why We Hate Us*," I say. "It is about the deterioration of American society and traditions and community. He says we are anchorless. He talks about people who speak loudly on their cell phones in public spaces about their colonoscopies and children who are basically marketing themselves on Facebook. There used to be lessons taught in school and at home about table manners and etiquette. We wanted to emulate families in *Good Housekeeping* magazine. We now worship actors and entertainers who use vulgarity to get attention and drugs to escape reality. He said there are no more have-tos. Men don't have to hold the door for women anymore. Companies don't have to retain their employees for thirty to forty years. Couples don't have to be married to have sex or to have children. Adult children don't have to care for their elderly parents anymore. Respect and loyalty are things of the past."

"It's become a me-me-me society," Lauren says while lowering the volume on the radio.

"Exactly, but no one is happier for it. All this me time leads to what? Being alone with your smartphone? We don't have a sense of belonging to a community anymore. They talk about a YouTube community? I'm sorry, but sharing videos on YouTube is not creating a community. It creates a socially incompetent individual who sits at his computer all day, looking at dog tricks, pornography, and celebrities behaving badly."

"It's really pathetic," she says.

We finally arrive at our hotel for the night. As we climb down from the truck and stretch our arms to the stars, exposing our belly buttons, Lauren's phone beeps again. She digs it out of her purse, reads the text, and growls.

I look at her as I open the door of the flatbed. "When my aunts would lament about being single, worried they'd never marry, my granny would say to them, 'For every little stocking, there is a little shoe.'"

Apparently, Granny Catherine believed in *sole* mates too.

Lauren smirks at me as she crawls up inside the truck to pull out her suitcase. "I think we're going to be barefoot for a while."

19

We're Off to See the Wizard—Judy Garland

As I eat a bagel with cream cheese the next morning in the tiny dining area off the lobby of the Sioux Falls hotel, the tables and chairs are suddenly swarming with a team of fifteen-year-old boys. Only two other adults are eating breakfast, so I assume they are the chaperones. We all stare at the television above the microwave until something comes on the screen that gives me the opportunity to begin a conversation with the strangers.

"Where are you all from?" I ask one of the female chaperones.

"About a six-hour drive from here on the opposite side of South Dakota," she replies.

"We came to Sioux Falls because the team here has a soccer game today," the other female chaperone adds.

"Are these your students?" I ask, looking at the boys, who seem well behaved, unless they are just exhausted from the journey or maybe stayed up all night watching television.

"Yes," the first teacher responds proudly.

"Aren't there high schools near your area to compete against?" I ask as Lauren joins me at the table with a cup of yogurt.

"No, but we're used to it. Everything is pretty spread out here, so you have to drive a long distance to do just about anything," the second teacher says matter-of-factly.

"Does the school have a budget to put this many students up in a hotel?" I am thinking of the recent budget cuts we experienced in New York City, one of the reasons I am jobless.

"No, we had to raise money for the trip. The parents pulled their dollars together for this one."

Both teachers smile with gratitude in the creases of their mouths.

"And where are you gals from?" the first teacher asks, changing the subject.

"New York City. We're on a road trip," Lauren says. "Tara is chasing her granny's spirit across America. We're headed to Seattle."

"Wow! Boys, do you hear that?" The teachers get the attention of the teenagers. "These girls are from New York City." The teachers look back at us with new enthusiasm, as if we are celebrities. "We've always wanted to go see a show on Broadway!"

"Well, we've always wanted to drive out west." I smile.

"Where are you headed next?" the second teacher asks.

"We have to get to Rapid City tonight. My granny went to Mount Rushmore."

"Oh, that's a ways. You have to cross the whole state," the teacher tells us as she finishes her coffee.

"But you can't miss Mitchell. And there's a car show today," the other teacher adds.

"Car show?" I ask as I stand up to throw out my garbage.

"Oh yes!" says one of the teachers as both perk up. "It's only an hour from here; it's on your way."

"And there will be old cars parked outside the Corn Palace. You just have to see the Corn Palace!"

I look at Lauren. "That's where my granny stopped."

"Then we have to go!" Lauren jumps up from the table.

The late September sun is blazing by high noon. It feels like a day in May, one they write poems about. I wonder if I'll ever need the wool sweaters I brought. Maybe Montana will be colder. We have a long drive ahead of us, but as the teachers exclaimed, we just have to stop in Mitchell. I tell Lauren we'll just take a look at the Corn Palace, grab a bite for lunch, perhaps find some corn on the cob, and then hit the road again. However, as we drive past the main street, which is closed to traffic, we catch a glimpse of the vintage cars parked in the middle of the road, one being a '57 Bel Air. We scream in unison. When I pull the Silverado into a spacious parking lot a few blocks from the Corn Palace, I turn the ignition off and look over at Lauren. "We may have to adjust our schedule."

This is exactly what Granny Catherine did on her road trip. She stopped when she saw something that caught her interest, and she lingered. Mount Rushmore wasn't going anywhere. Roosevelt and Lincoln could wait.

It's Saturday. The main street reminds me of a Memorial Day celebration, with families strolling by with ice cream cones, soda pop, baseball caps, and bicycles. Farmers in flannel shirts stand next to cowboys in ten-gallon hats. Teenagers have tattoos and T-shirts depicting Chevrolet and Route 66 logos.

A temporary sound stage set up inside an eighteen-wheeler sits in the center of town, with a live band playing "Rock This Town" by the Stray Cats as locals sit listening and tapping their toes on the curbside. I throw my handbag onto the ground and grab Lauren's arm, and we begin swing dancing in front of the crowd. She screams like a schoolgirl, and when the song ends, we're both out of breath, but we receive a nice round of applause from the locals.

"You girls sure look like you know what yer doin'." An old farmer smiles at us from the curb.

We continue to walk down Main Street past antique automobiles for five or six blocks as the boulevard becomes an outdoor museum for car enthusiasts, taking photos and reading the placards inside each window. We see 1929 Fords, 1937 Chevrolets, 1949 Oldsmobiles, 1952 Plymouths, 1969 Pontiacs, and 1971 Chevy Novas. Every decade is represented, as is every make and model of American engineering.

The most popular car on the block, with the largest number of vehicles parked in front of saloons, cafés, and jewelry shops whose facades look as if they haven't changed since the middle of the previous century, is the Bel Air—and not just the 1957 model but the 1955 and 1956 models as well. The Tri-Fives, they were called.

It is a Bel Air buffet. I have never seen so many Bel Airs. Usually, Memorial Day parades or car shows have one or maybe two, but now, block after block, there are dozens and dozens of them, some in mint condition and others exposing rusted roots, showing their age. I am in no rush to get back on the road as my hungry eyes devour every detail.

My eyes are suddenly drawn to a shiny black 1957 convertible Corvette with a red interior. Standing next to it is an equally attractive young man in his early twenties.

"Louise!" I call to Lauren. "Look! This might be our Brad Pitt."

We approach the young blond as he stands proudly next to his dream machine.

"I'm Tara." I extend my hand. "This is Lauren."

She smiles and tilts her red head, shading her eyes with her hand. "But you can call us Thelma and Louise." Lauren is always the flirt.

"I'm Dustin, and this is Cody." He motions to his friend beside him with casual coolness. Their names couldn't be more perfect. We convince Dustin to let me sit in his car with him for a brief photo shoot. He obliges with the manners of a midwesterner. He even opens the car door for me.

As Lauren sets up her shots, Cody watches her from under his baseball cap.

"Act natural. Conversate," Lauren says, directing from behind her lens.

"So you own this gorgeous vehicle?" I smile at Dustin, trying to distract him from Lauren's interfering lens.

"Uh, yeah, and I also own a 1969 Camaro and a 1979 Corvette." He tries to act casual and places his hand on the steering wheel, squinting at me under the midday sun.

"If you could go anywhere in the USA in your Chevrolet, where would you like to go?"

"Vegas," he responds without hesitation.

I don't want to get out of this glass slipper. I want Dustin to take me for a ride so I can feel the wind in my hair. I imagine us going for a drive down a country lane and picnicking on a blanket under a shady tree. He looks like he really would take me to Vegas. But being a cougar is not my intention, so I force myself to climb out of the Corvette.

We thank Dustin for his time, and we leave him with Cody and continue to explore the curbside gallery, wondering how a young man like that could afford to own so many classic cars, collecting them like fine pieces of art. We see him and his friend trailing us throughout the afternoon. We must have made an impression on them as well.

I try to interview an even younger man who is cleaning valves, knobs, and other shiny bits of this and that under the hood of his '57 Chevy Bel Air, but he isn't very communicative. All I get out of the sixteen-year-old is that he owns the vehicle, and his father, a mechanic, owns the 1959 Chevy parked beside his. Perhaps he is shy, and my curiosity is intimidating. I simply want to learn more about his Chevy. He most likely fell in love with his car because his dad shared the same passion. He grew up around them, I suppose.

As I reveal some of my story about my granny's road trip to him and his equally reserved father, an older gentleman is standing by, peering under the hood but listening to my every word. His age gives him the confidence to converse with me further. He was a music professor, he informs me.

"Taught for forty years." He smiles proudly.

"Would you sing for us?" I ask the former choral instructor. I want to record all sorts of Americans singing Dinah Shore's version of "See the USA in Your Chevrolet." I know this gentleman is capable, and he doesn't appear to be shy since he was the one who approached us.

"I'd be delighted." Professor Pete beams as I get on one knee and record him with the backdrop of the famous Corn Palace above him.

He sings the song and holds up his jazz hands for a little extra pizzazz. I instruct him to only sing one line of the advertisement so that I can edit his part with other Americans singing the song that is now lodged in my brain and won't let me sleep at night.

"Did you see inside the Corn Palace yet?" Professor Pete points to the historic building behind us.

"No, is it worth it?" I ask as I put away my video camera.

"Oh sure, it's a part of American history. They built it in 1892 to encourage people to settle in this area. And the exterior decor is changed every year by an artist. They create the murals using real cobs of corn," he says with pride under a sign that reads, "American Pride."

"We'll have to check it out. But first we have to eat."

I shade the sun from my eyes, searching for my copilot, and I see her taking a picture of the grille of another Chevy.

"Go get a burger across the street there." He points to an outdoor eatery. "They have the best burgers in town."

Granny Catherine ordered her first burger with everything at a roadside diner. After that initial bite, my dad said he and his mother and sister Peg ordered burgers with everything every chance they could on the road. They'd never eaten meat between two pieces of bread piled with pickles, lettuce, tomatoes, onions, ketchup, and mustard and dripping with the juice of grade-A beef. They said their taste buds died and went to heaven.

I thank the professor and grab Lauren, and we make our way across the street and ask for a table outside under an umbrella. It's too darn hot inside the bar. However, we begin to regret our decision when the bees and flies start to hover over our sodas and ketchup bottle.

"I recall my aunt saying they ate lunch at a place across the street from the Corn Palace," I say to Lauren as she sits slumped in her chair, checking emails on her phone. We spent the entire afternoon walking the town under the sun without food or water. She doesn't have the energy to answer me.

Suddenly, Professor Pete appears again. We invite him to join us, but he says he's already eaten.

"However, I'll sit for a spell, as I don't get to chat with too many New Yorkers in this neck of the woods."

As Professor Pete speaks about his long teaching career and interest in the arts, I think of my granduncle, the one Granny was on her way to visit in Spokane, Washington. He taught at Gonzaga University. His name was Peter too.

"Aren't we artsy people great?" he says as Lauren and I swat away the bees encroaching on our corn on the cob bathed in butter. The burgers aren't as good as the ones Dad raved about. Professor Pete continues to share stories, and we slowly regain our energy. "I brought my students to see *Wicked* on Broadway ten times."

"Now, that is a seriously long distance for a field trip to see the Wicked Witch of the West. There are students in the Bronx who have never even been to Broadway," I tell him.

"It was worth it," he says, ignoring the bees and my comments about distance. "The arts are always worth it."

I look at the yellow facade of the Corn Palace behind the white hairs on Professor Pete's head. I think of the journey between Mitchell, South Dakota, and Times Square. I am reminded of the yellow brick road and people who dream, and I wonder what is on the other side of the rainbow. "Follow," I hear the wind whisper to me. "Follow that road."

20

Badlands—Bruce Springsteen

"You're going too fast," my father tells me when he finds me with his finger on his map of America as we leave Mitchell, South Dakota, in the late-afternoon sun.

"No, we're not," I say. "We spent the whole day in that small town."

"You're approaching the best part of the country. All you're going to see is the highway if you keep up this pace. You've got to get off the road. Where do you plan on staying tonight?" he asks, concerned I am not experiencing the leisurely journey he experienced since he didn't have to return the car within a specified period of time.

"We want to get to Rapid City so we can see Mount Rushmore." I am looking at a map as Lauren is driving. I finally relinquished the wheel.

"No, you're going to miss one of my favorite parts of the trip. You have to find a town closer to the Badlands and explore that for a day."

I can hear his finger on his map. I can also hear his envy. He wanted to come with me on this trip. He wanted to relive one of the greatest summers of his life, one of the last times he spent quality time with his mother, who died soon after he returned from the army. But I wanted to re-create *Thelma and Louise*, minus the suicidal launch into the Grand Canyon. Dad secretly hoped Lauren would back out at the last minute, but she was just as excited about the opportunity as if it had been her family adventure, and besides, I figured I'd attract more attention from cowboys with a cute redhead by my side rather than my aging father. Though, now that I think about it, I should have taken my dad. It would have been an amazing father-daughter experience.

But he is always with us. If I don't call him first thing in the morning, the phone will ring. "Where are my travelers today?" he sings into the phone.

He always expects a call at night and worries if we drive in the dark. He asks how we got on that day, following me with his finger. I am also keeping a blog for myself and for Chevrolet. No matter how late at night we arrive at our hotel, Lauren and I spend at least two hours uploading images and videos. We know we have an eager audience. Dad and Aunt Peg turn their computers on first thing in the morning to read our blogs before they even make coffee. Some locations don't have Wi-Fi, and in those cases, they contact us by nine o'clock in the morning to ask why they didn't receive a new post.

Dad suggests we find a hotel in the town of Wall. It's on the edge of the Badlands, and we can explore the national park early the next morning. A farmer at a gas station 120 miles east of Wall recommends we go to the town's famous drugstore to taste their homemade maple-frosted doughnuts.

"But you'll have to hurry," he says. "They close at seven."

As we race across the flat plains, testing the speedometer of the Silverado, we notice one billboard after the next. Wall Drugstore advertises for about three hundred miles: "Wall Donuts, Best in the West! Wall Western Gear, Saddle Up! You're Almost at Wall!" The anticipation is killing us. We just have to try those doughnuts, and their coffee is only five cents. Five cents? Take that, Starbucks.

I am curious to learn why this drugstore is known for miles and miles, so I google the establishment and read about the original owners, Dorothy and Ted Hustead, a married couple who opened the store in 1931 in a prairie town with a population of only 326 people. They couldn't get the locals to come to their store because the residents were just too poor. Potential customers were driving from east to west, and Dorothy wondered how she could come up with a way to coerce them to take a detour to their store, which was well off the beaten path. Then one day she had an idea. She told her husband they should advertise free ice water. She knew the travelers were hot and thirsty, and she also knew that if they came into the store, they'd enjoy the free ice water and stay for a slice of her pie just out of the oven or an ice cream sundae with fresh cream.

So they made a sign on the highway, which was more of a dirt road at the time, and suddenly, people were flocking to the store. They eventually attracted so many customers they had to expand their small shop, which still has rails outside to tie up horses. The Wall Drugstore is now so popular with travelers that its dining room has seating for 530 occupants, with twenty thousand visitors per day, and the original shop extends into a minimall that sells everything from cowboy boots to Native American jewelry. It even has a narrow little chapel where one can sit for a spell and pray for a safe journey.

The lesson Dorothy learned is that no place is godforsaken. Everyone has the ability to succeed, no matter where he or she lives or what he or she does for a living, especially if the incentive is to serve others. I wonder if this Dorothy owned a pair of ruby-red slippers too.

We finally arrive in Wall a few minutes before closing. We park on a dusty road lined with shops under a wooden canopy and make our way inside. There are only two doughnuts left on the counter, and Lauren and I pounce on them. We regret lingering so long at the car show and Corn Palace that afternoon when we see the labyrinth of shops closing down for the night.

After we purchase our cherished doughnuts, a salesperson puts up a velvet rope to make sure no other customers enter the dining area. We make our way outside to the wooden sidewalk, looking for a bench to enjoy our dinner of doughnuts, when I notice railroad tracks across the road. As we watch the sun set behind a handful of houses, we stand on the tracks, waiting to see if a train will come.

Our ears ache as we listen for a whistle, but we hear only crickets welcoming the night with their song.

My dad's parents lived a few blocks from the Long Island Railroad tracks when they moved from the Bronx to Queens. I remember walking to the Little Neck station and putting pennies on the rail, hoping to see a train flatten one of them. My father did the same in the 1950s with his sister Peg, whom he called Joe. He always wanted a brother.

I didn't know then, when I placed pennies on the tracks as a child, that Granny Catherine fainted at that Little Neck train station years before I was born. An African American woman gave her some gin to revive her as she lay on the platform. My grandfather took her to the hospital later that day, where they learned she had an advanced stage of colon cancer. She didn't want to die in the hospital, so she spent her last days in their small home, where, when I would visit as a child, Granddad permitted me to drink one can of his ginger ale and eat one of his store-bought oatmeal cookies but only if I stayed in the kitchen.

My memories of that stale house only contain my grandfather, with furnishings that hadn't been updated since the fifties. Both he and the furnishings seemed trapped in time. Granny Catherine was there in that house, but I didn't know it—in the wallpaper, the blue bathroom tiles, and the china cabinet, where her Waterford crystal collected dust against a wall in the living room. The basement, with its low ceilings and linoleum floor, where she'd held many parties, was filled with dark shadows rather than her laughter. It didn't feel like my Donegal grandparents' home at all. Perhaps a woman singing in the kitchen keeps a house fresh, makes the wallpaper more vivid, and puts a smile on an old man's face, no matter how much his bones remind him of his age.

I didn't like going to Granddad's house in Little Neck. I felt as if I were in his way. I remember avoiding him by playing in the basement, where I saw triangular felt banners on the walls, like university flags. They read, "Yellowstone," "Butte America," and

"Wyoming." Granny Catherine bought the souvenirs during her road trip in 1957. I didn't know at the time what they signified. My grandfather never took them down. They were a reminder of his wife's first taste of freedom.

I had a dream about him recently. He stood smiling like a child, waiting to go up to the light at the top of the stairs. I embraced him heartily in the dream and whispered words I never uttered when he was alive: "I love you." Then he disappeared into the light.

"It's getting dark," Lauren calls, bringing me out of my memories, as we follow the railroad tracks back to the Silverado and on to our hotel for the evening.

Lauren sits in the Silverado as I check into our hotel in Wall. A smile greets me before I even open the glass door to the main office. There stands a young man named Joseph.

"Welcome!" He beams from behind the counter. "Are you Tara?" he asks, still smiling.

"Wow! Are you psychic?" I'm thrown by his assumption.

"Oh no." He suddenly becomes self-conscious, looking down at his shoes. "It's just that we have no vacancy, and everyone has checked in for the night, and you are the last customer with a reservation to check in."

"But it's only eight o'clock." I look at my watch. "Everyone is in bed already?"

"Oh sure, people rise early to get a head start on the Badlands or to drive wherever they are going. Besides, there's not much to do here at night."

"Yeah, I realized that when the drugstore closed at seven. I got the last doughnut."

"Oh, aren't they just wonderful? Did you try the maple or the chocolate?" He says everything like a child in Santa's workshop. Every word, no matter how simple, is enchanted.

"Maple," I answer, trying to determine if he is genuine. "But my friend and I missed the rest of the menu."

"Oh, well, you can go back for breakfast," he says. "They open fairly early. Though we serve a complimentary breakfast here, and you are welcome to eat in our dining room."

I peek into the dining room off to the left of the main entrance. I then glance around the lobby. It doesn't feel like the other hotels. There are small accents of wood, wind chimes, and music, which make it feel like a day spa.

"I like the decor in here," I say, admiring a print behind his desk.

"Well, thank you very much. I take that as a great compliment. I did all the woodwork. I'm also the owner of the hotel," he says proudly as the phone rings. "Oh, please excuse me, Tara." He politely holds up his finger as he answers the phone and proceeds to speak in the most delightful manner.

"Best of the West. Oh, hello! Yes, that would be fine. Oh, sure you can. Aw, now, thanks. You have yourself a great evening. Okay now. Bye-bye."

I examine his face. "How old are you, if you don't mind me asking?"

"I don't mind at all. I'm twenty-five." He nods as if confirming to himself.

I keep meeting twenty-something-year-olds with their own businesses. I realize there is more I want to learn about this young man. He has honesty in his eyes that a New Yorker doesn't recognize, and I want to hear more about his life in Wall, South Dakota. I can tell he has a story he is itching to share, so I get a room key, help Lauren check in with our numerous bags, and then return to the office with a Chevy poster and one of my CDs. I decide if I am going to interview people, I should at least give them something in return.

Joseph does have a story to tell, and his openness floors me. It's amazing what happens when you ask people what their dreams are. It's as if you are giving them permission to dream.

He says he grew up on a Native American reservation. He helped his family raise cattle and horses and was a "typical farm boy." He drove fifty miles each way to his high school. People didn't expect him to graduate, not even his teachers, but he had ambition and wanted to move away from the reservation and small town to go to college.

When he was born, his family registered him as Caucasian despite his Native American ancestry because with his blond bangs, he looked more like a Northern European than a member of the Lakota Nation. When a relative who was registered as a Native American was offered college scholarship money, Joseph was heartbroken. He worked multiple jobs to pay for his own education and decided he should study as far away from home as he could.

He applied to a college in Hawaii. He didn't have a place to live, as it was a commuter school, but he met a family on the plane, and during the flight, the family decided to take him under their wing and let him move in with them. I believe his magical and enchanting discourse makes strangers feel like family in his presence. This determined, personable, and spiritual individual eventually came back to South Dakota. He couldn't deny where he came from. He admits his ancestors fought on both sides of the battle at Wounded Knee.

What is his dream? He wants to return to Hawaii, where the people and the ocean welcomed him warmly, and live each day as if it is his last. He also wants to marry a nice girl and have children. He believes that someone is watching out for him up above and that he has lived many lives, perhaps in Hawaii, as it keeps beckoning him.

"That's funny because I feel like Montana has been beckoning me all my life," I tell him as he smiles. "I always felt this urge to go there, but I don't know why."

"Perhaps it has been calling you in the wind or in your dreams. You must have a purpose there." His smile never fades when he speaks.

"Perhaps, and I also feel that someone is watching over me." I think of Granny Nora, and Joseph smiles as we share a sacred moment in the lobby of a hotel on the edge of the Badlands.

I give him a copy of my CD to thank him for his time and for sharing his story, and then he disappears into a back room and returns with a DVD.

"This is my favorite film. I watch it all the time. It's called *Thunder Heart*. Have you seen it?"

"No." I look at an image of Val Kilmer on the cover.

"Watch this, and you will know where I come from. It will help you understand what life was like growing up on a reservation. Just note that it's not a feel-good movie."

"Is there a DVD player in my room?"

"No, you can keep it. It's my thank-you gift to you."

"I can't take your favorite film," I say.

"Please do. I really enjoyed speaking with you, and your granny story is inspiring. You've given me something to think about. I'm going to listen to your music tonight and make a list of the things I want to do and places I want to go. I don't meet many people like you very often in South Dakota. Actually, I've never met anyone like you."

"I get that a lot."

I bid Joseph good night and cautiously exit the lobby through the glass door, closing it quickly, as if I am containing butterflies in a greenhouse.

Lauren and I wake before the rattlesnakes. We want to be in Badlands National Park just as it opens at eight o'clock. The park ranger at the ticket booth informs us that we are the first to arrive. We have all 244,000 acres to ourselves, and it is only 7:57 a.m. Well, we aren't entirely alone. There are a handful of bison, bighorn sheep, prairie dogs, and black-footed ferrets where rhinos and saber-toothed cats once roamed, but we only see a herd of deer on the road.

After we park at the first scenic viewpoint, I step to the edge of the terrain, beyond the safety railing, beyond the Beware of Rattlesnakes sign, until my foot comes dangerously close to the rock formation that drops into the canyon below. My eyes search the distance where the rock dips into gullies and ravines, where my granny stood and took snapshots of a landscape she described as looking like the face of the moon. I record the stillness and silence of the scene on video, interrupted only by the sound of crickets and a lone butterfly that dances in front of my lens.

I think of Joseph's great-grandparents, who crossed these lands on horseback. He revealed he is a descendant of both the American soldiers and the victims they massacred at Wounded Knee forty-five miles from this site as the inhabitants sang and danced themselves into a trance, assembling in the hundreds, frightening the white men, who didn't understand their ghost dance. The Lakota people believed wisdom came to them in dreams. Their prophets spread messages of hope with visions of peace. Dance, they were told. Their dance became religion. Their dance sent them to the spirit world, where Joseph's grandparents are now dancing with my grandparents at the crossroads of the Universe.

This is a challenging environment to grow up in, I think to myself, looking out at the land the Native Americans called bad. It's so different from my concrete canyons in New York. Although we were both born in America, I realize from his stories shared over the counter in the hotel lobby that Joseph and I have two different perspectives of America. I was born of a Celtic tribe, and he was born of a Native one. I grew up within reach of the ocean, and he grew up in a barren, dry, and landlocked place. But the voices of our ancestors empty into our eardrums as the wind sweeps across the land, both good and bad.

Speak to me, Granny.

21

Stars Fell on Alabama—Ella Fitzgerald and Louis Armstrong

Lauren and I pull into the parking lot of a Rapid City hotel we booked only a few hours before on the highway. There was no reception in the Badlands. We were disconnected for hours. But we didn't care because each curve in the road led us to a new vista, and we jumped out of the truck almost every quarter of a mile to take a photo or just take in the scene. Lauren giggles to herself as she scans through the images on her camera when I turn the ignition off.

"Every picture is of you jumping." She laughs, leaning over to show me one of my favorite images so far from the road trip. I look like a cheerleader, with my arms and legs extended in an X. Lauren was lying on the ground when she took the low-angle shot. I'm at least two feet off the ground, with my head thrown back and my mouth wide open. Her camera captured the colors exceptionally well, from the cloudless deep blue sky above me to the tall golden grass alongside me. The image captured the joy I felt in that moment, a response to the feelings of freedom and discovery the journey is giving me and the excitement and anticipation of waking up each morning and wondering, *What will I see today? Whom will I meet?*

Every day should feel like that, I think to myself.

"Come on. I'm starving," I say finally as Lauren keeps scanning the images.

We explored the Badlands, Mount Rushmore, and the Black Hills in one day. We haven't eaten since having a snack under Abraham Lincoln's nose, and it is already ten o'clock at night.

After we check into the hotel, we make our way across the street, where we see a diner. It's called Arnold's, like the one in *Happy Days*, and when we walk inside, Lauren and I gasp and grab each other's forearms. The grille and front portion of the body of an actual '57 Chevy Bel Air make up the base of the counter in the 1950s-themed diner.

"Lauren! Oh my God, this is amazing." I drool while scanning the menu. The entire menu is Chevrolet themed. There's a Chevy Burger, a Malibu Burger, a Corvette Burger, and even a chili burger called the Stingray. When we booked the hotel from our phone on the highway, we had no idea a Bel Air diner would be directly across the street.

She must be guiding us, I think to myself as a waiter leads us to a booth.

Lauren and I look at each other. We don't need words. We know what is happening. Her eyes say, *Can you believe this?*

My eyes reply, *Actually, yes!* Then our eyes follow a towering plate of beef, vegetables, and mashed potatoes swimming in an ocean of gravy, and we sink deeper into our booth, weak with hunger, exhaustion, and the excitement of the day.

Mount Rushmore was an interesting tourist site, built only for the purpose of bringing tourists and their money to the area, just like the Corn Palace. It was the first time we felt we were at an actual tourist site because of the large parking lots, lines, and entrance fees. I didn't realize we would be able to get so close to the monument. I also didn't realize it was initially supposed to be a sculpture of Native American leaders, but the artist refused to put up Pocahontas. He wanted the US presidents, our Seth Rogen–look-alike park ranger told us as he led us under the nose of Teddy Roosevelt.

I imagined seeing Cary Grant climb around the faces of each president, as the actor did in Hitchcock's *North by Northwest*, as Seth explained that the land we stood on was still being fought over in the courts to this day. A US-government treaty gave the land to the Native Americans, but the government took it back when the white men discovered gold in them there hills.

There was a busload of Japanese tourists taking photos of the monument. It was the first time since Chicago I had seen people who didn't look as if they were descendants from Northern Europe. I'm so used to diversity in New York and the major cities that it's strange for me to see only one flavor out west.

When Lauren and I needed a break from the heat of the midafternoon sun, we stepped into the dining hall at the tourist center for some ice cream. Interestingly, they only had vanilla to offer us, as their chocolate fountain was broken. As I said, there's mostly one flavor in the Midwest.

I suggested we go see Crazy Horse, a Native American memorial still being carved into another mountain in the Black Hills. In 1939, Henry Standing Bear stated that he and his fellow chiefs would like the white man to know that the red man has great heroes also. Crazy Horse is remembered for how he cared for the elderly, the ill, the widowed, and children. He devoted his life to serving his people and preserving their valued culture.

Your worth is determined by your service to others.

But as we drove the winding road lined with trees and rose higher and higher into the Black Hills, blinded by the late-afternoon sun, we wondered if we'd ever find Crazy Horse. That was when we found Trevor and Sarah from Alabama climbing off their motorcycle at a scenic viewpoint. Trevor looked like an even better-looking version of Kenny Rogers with his white hair and beard. His wife, Sarah, was ethereal with her long blonde hair. We all examined the You Are Here sign posted on a visitors' guide to the area, when we got to talking.

After I explained the purpose for my road trip, Trevor revealed that he worked for General Motors for thirty-one years. Now that he was retired, he and his lovely wife were fulfilling a lifelong dream: driving an RV around America for an entire year.

"We're taking a pause to reinvent ourselves on the road." He looked lovingly into his wife's kind, receptive eyes. "We also wanted to take time to appreciate our relationship for a richer and more meaningful marriage," he added as she leaned into him and put her head on his shoulder.

"I think I'm gonna cry." Lauren dabbed the edge of her eye, holding back tears.

We stood for forty-five minutes in that parking lot, talking about life, dreams, America, and everything in between. We hadn't even seen the scenic view yet, the reason we'd stopped our vehicles, but we didn't care. We were thoroughly enjoying the spontaneous conversation about the meaning of life in a parking lot in the Black Hills of South Dakota with strangers from Alabama who felt more like family with each admission.

"Fifty percent of happiness comes from what you do for a living and what you give to your community. That gives you purpose," Alabama Trevor said. "Another twenty-five percent of happiness comes from your family."

"What does the last twenty-five percent represent?" I asked this wise soul.

"Football, hot dogs, and beer. It's the simple things in life."

We all laughed heartily as his wife suggested we look at the view before the sun set.

We walked to the edge of the cliff and climbed up rugged rocks to get beyond the evergreens. As we sat admiring the tops of the trees, Sarah opened up to me.

"I was born with a feeling that I had to keep going and get out there to see the world. It was always my dream to travel in an RV. It represents freedom for us. We can just get up and go wherever we want or stay and linger in a place if we'd like."

Trevor came closer to our platform. "Yeah, we've been in the Black Hills for three weeks now because we just love this area so much. We only bought the bike yesterday so we could feel the wind in our hair and enjoy the curves in these roads."

"Driving around and exploring helps us connect to nature and the Creator. Plus, we get to meet great people like you!" Sarah touched my arm as we headed back to the parking lot. There was healing in those hands.

We took a few photos together, and they even sang "See the USA in Your Chevrolet" for my video camera. After numerous hugs and warm wishes, Trevor and Sarah climbed back onto their newly purchased motorcycle.

"You gals sure make life fun! Meeting you both makes us feel good to be alive!" Alabama Trevor's tone was so sincere it was my turn to start crying.

"Slow down, and enjoy," he called to us as Sarah wrapped her arms around his waist, leaning into his frame, reminding me of my grandparents, who met at a crossroads dance and shared a bicycle home. At first, I thought Alabama Trevor was referring to our road trip, but then he added one more bumper sticker as he revved the bike and zoomed out of the parking lot and into the wilderness of the Black Hills.

"Life goes by too fast!" he called from a distance with his Kenny Rogers beard.

I like his pause-button philosophy, especially in our age of remote control.

22

Even Cowgirls Get the Blues— Emmylou Harris

Cowgirl is an attitude, really. A pioneer spirit, a special American brand of courage. The cowgirl faces life head on, lives by her own lights, makes no excuses. Cowgirls take stands. They speak up. They defend things they hold dear. A cowgirl might be a rancher, or a barrel racer, or a bull rider, or an actress. But she's just as likely to be a checker at the local Winn Dixie, a full-time mother, a banker, an attorney, or an astronaut.

—Dale Evans, Queen of the Cowgirls

As we drive across Wyoming, I fall in love with the inspiring landscape that beckoned early frontiersmen and women who migrated west in search of wide-open spaces and better lives with the hope of finding gold in them there hills. My aunt Peg calls to check on our location, and when I tell her where we are on the map, she says, "Try to imagine what it was like crossing those trails in covered wagons."

I can't imagine it. My survival skills involve knowing how to dial 911. I can't light a fire. I'm petrified of the gigantic water bugs in my apartment, let alone wolves or bears. I've only ever fired a gun once in my life, at a shooting range. The handgun terrified me, and my hands shook so much I could barely aim at the target. Surprisingly, the rifle felt more comfortable and steady in my grasp, giving me the confidence to hit the target. I experienced a feeling of empowerment at learning a new skill; however, firearms still scare the hell out of me. I don't even enjoy water pistols.

Aunt Peg informed me of a western art museum they toured in Cody with sculptures of Native Americans on horseback and paintings of cowboys on bucking broncos. Lauren and I race across yet another state to get to the Buffalo Bill Historical Center before closing to view the same works of art my granny saw.

When we pull into the crowded parking lot at a quarter to five, the only spot available is next to a red '57 Chevy Bel Air. *Seriously?* Granny Catherine's spirit is definitely laying out bread crumbs across the country.

We enter the historic center, which replaced the original museum housed in a log cabin, and Walter, the ticket agent, informs us the galleries are closing for the night.

"Oh no, Walter, you have to let us in. We just drove the entire state of Wyoming to see the western art my granny saw on her visit here in 1957," I say, pleading with the elderly gentleman.

"We're on a mission, Walt!" Lauren gives him her golden smile.

"You won't be able to see very much; this is a rather large center with numerous galleries," the disgruntled senior tells us, wondering why we drove hundreds of miles with only fifteen minutes to spare. Americans did that sort of traveling in Europe, seeing one country per day, zipping through the Louvre on their way to the Vatican.

"We just want to see the original exhibit my granny saw, just a peek, even if it's only a few minutes," I say with desperation in my voice.

The old man graciously waves the fifteen-dollar entrance fee so we can wander through one of the galleries for just a few precious minutes.

My heart races as we enter the dimly lit air-conditioned gallery. I want to devour every inch of it, but I know we don't have time. I'm not slowing down, as Alabama Trevor advised, but there is so much ground to cover in such a short period of time. I want to see and do everything Granny experienced on her road trip. I feel as if I am competing against a clock in a reality show.

I come upon a painting in the lofty gallery that helps me imagine the early pioneer women Aunt Peg was referring to. It is an oil painting of a woman sitting in a covered wagon and holding the leather reins. She is wearing a maroon dress with a white lace collar, and a red shawl is draped around her waist. She has a peaceful yet melancholic look on her face. The light coming through the back of the covered wagon outlines her red hair, creating the look of a halo around her angelic face. The wagon cover extends around her sides like the wings of an angel. I wonder if she lost her newborn or if she was a young widow. Was her vision of freedom different from the one she was experiencing on the open trail? What did she sacrifice to be there at that moment? I look at the title before I move on: *Madonna of the Prairie*, by W. H. D. Koerner, painted in 1921.

An announcement comes on a loudspeaker. The museum is closing in five minutes. I run across to another gallery featuring Buffalo Bill Cody himself, the man the town was named after. Saddles, firearms, clothing, and leather accessories as well as a life-sized wagon are on display. Then I discover Annie Oakley, who, during her time, was superior to most men on the shooting range. She became an international star in Buffalo Bill's rodeo show. She was a sharp broad, tough as nails.

On the wall is a quote attributed to Buffalo Bill Cody in 1899: "What we want to do is give our women even more liberty than they have. Let them do any kind of work that they see fit, and if they do it as well as men, give them the same pay."

I am starting to like Mr. Cody, who I learn was a frontiersman, a showman, the town founder, and an American icon.

Interestingly, the *New York Times* disagreed with him. As one reporter wrote in the May 27 edition of 1876, "Any woman who thirsts to wear trousers and ride broncos is a victim of a curious mental disorder."

I must be crazy then, because I am downright parched when it comes to wanting to pull on my brown corduroy pants each morning and climb up into my bucking Silverado. I usually wear makeup, a dress or a skirt, and heels when I go out in New York City, so putting on the same pair of worn-out, dirty trousers every day and not worrying about my hair or makeup on the road feels liberating. I'm not interested in impressing anyone, but I am interested in riding a horse.

As we wave goodbye to old Walt, thanking him for our short visit, we decide we should stay at a dude ranch while in Cody. My dad and aunt rode horses during their road trip, so we have to do the same, despite my severe allergy. Online, we find a ranch owned by a Texan family close to the west gate of Yellowstone.

We sit in the cozy dining room of the Cody ranch, waiting for our trout, broccoli, and medley of blue and sweet roasted potatoes. I suddenly hear hooves on the dirt pavement outside and catch a glimpse of the back of a mysterious cowboy racing up the lane with urgency.

"Oh, that's just Luke returning the horses from the last ride." Our waitress, Lorna, notices Lauren and me straining to see out the narrow slit in the windows through the quaint curtains. We reserved our ride for the morning, as we decided to use Alabama Trevor's pause button for the night.

"Maybe he's our Brad Pitt, Thelma," Lauren says as she digs into her blue medley.

"Will he be our guide in the morning?" I ask Lorna as she peers out the window.

"It'll be either him or Chase. They're fighting over who gets to go on the last ride of the season," she says, still looking out the window. "Is that your Silverado?"

"Yes. Well, I don't own it. Chevy gave it to me to take this road trip."

"They just gave you a truck for nothin'?" She almost drops the pitcher of water she is carrying.

"I have to return it, but yes. Actually, I asked for the loan of it for free." I proceed to tell her the story of my granny quest going west.

"I used to pray for a horse for free," Lorna says. "Ever since I was five years old, I wanted a horse. Then, one day a few years ago, a man who knew my family made that dream come true. I named her Roxy. I don't know what I like best—riding Roxy or driving my Silverado."

"You drive a Silverado too?" Lauren looks up from her trout.

"Sure, Texan girls love their Chevys."

After dinner, we move into the living room area to digest and examine the fireplace and rustic artifacts within the main log cabin. The front desk where we checked in has a jar of homemade chocolate chip cookies. The owner sees me peeking at the jar and says I can take one if I'd like.

"We also have ingredients for s'mores out by the fire pit," she adds.

I look at Lauren with raised eyebrows.

"You know the answer to that question," she says, reading my face.

I remain near the front desk and notice someone inside an office, sitting at a computer.

"Louise," I whisper to Lauren, "look."

Our Brad Pitt–look-alike cowboy is examining an image of a curly-haired brunette standing beside a '57 Chevy Bel Air.

"Hey, that's me!" I'm shocked, recognizing my photo.

The cowboy spins around on his chair and saunters into the dimly lit lobby.

"You're looking at my blog?" I ask as he smiles shyly and shoves his hands into his denim pockets.

"Lorna told us all about your Chevy trip," the woman behind the desk says. "We each own a Silverado. I'm Trish. My husband, Bill, and I run the ranch."

Introductions continue around the room as we meet her son, Chase, and his wife, Becca, who join us in the lobby.

"I'm Luke." The young cowboy finally extends his firm hand. I can barely see his blues eyes under the black cowboy hat covering his long dirty-blond hair.

Yes, Louise, we've found our Brad Pitt. And I want to ride off into the sunset with him.

Luke is from Georgia. He graduated from college six months before and decided to begin a journey similar to mine.

"My grandmother drove a Chevy across country in 1996." His voice is like a southern wind gently playing with the peaches ripening on the branches of a Georgian tree. "Her stories inspired me. She used to take me to the depot to watch the trains go by, and I was always curious to know where people were going. I have her atlas outlining her route from her road trip."

"I have the exact route my granny took in 1957!" I exclaim, delighted we have something in common, if not age. "I've been stopping everywhere she went. She always wanted to see the Wild West, as she called it."

I watch his face change as the excitement of the idea takes over.

"I wanna do the same but not just across the US. I wanna go west across the world. And not in a Chevy," he says. "I'm gonna do it on a horse."

"Wow! How are you going to do that?" I say, stealing glances at his muscular arms and imagining riding across the world with him, wrapping my arms around his broad frame, and picking out a pair of cowgirl boots to match his.

"Well, I'll obviously take boats across the ocean, but each place I go, I will ride and work on ranches." He adjusts his hat and folds his arms across his chest as he leans into a pillar.

"So where do you plan to go next?" Lauren has been eying him from behind. He has the attention of every woman in the room.

"Now that the ranch is closing for winter, I wanna go to New Zealand next and then head to Japan, Southeast Asia, the Middle East, and India. I think I might wanna ride elephants in India."

"That's an amazing idea. So you leave for New Zealand tomorrow?" I unconsciously fold my arms across my chest, mimicking his stance, wishing I brought my passport with me.

At this question, Luke looks down. The Texan family gathered in the lobby wait on his words. When he looks up again, his eyes are filled with oceans of feeling.

"No, I have to head back to Georgia." He pauses until he can manage to explain. "My grandmother died yesterday."

Trish puts her hand to her mouth. "Luke, you didn't tell us that was the reason you were flying home." Her motherly voice soothes the silence.

I want to touch his arm. I recognize the suffering in his eyes, the slow ache that surfaces with each memory of watching trains go by, hearing songs in the pantry, and knowing we won't have our grandmothers forever but wishing with all our might we could be the one exception.

"I suffered a great deal when I lost my granny in Ireland," I say as Luke nods and adjusts his cowboy hat over his eyes. "I never met the grandmother whose spirit I'm chasing now. But I feel her with me everyday." I reach out and finally touch his arm. "It's good that you're going home, and it's also good that you're going west in honor of her journey."

At this, Luke smiles politely and then excuses himself from the room. He says he has to pack his bags for the morning. Trish watches him walk away.

"He received a letter from his grandmother today in the mail. It was sent a week ago." She shakes her head in disbelief and retreats behind the desk.

Lauren and I escape the heavy air of the main cabin and make our way to the fire pit, where we find marshmallows, chocolate squares, and graham crackers. I watch the flames dance and feel the familiar warmth of the bonfires my grandfather lit in his field on the farm in Donegal on the night of the summer solstice. I remember the sting of the drizzle on my face the morning Granny Nora died and the last letter I wrote to her, the one she didn't get to read because she had already slipped into a comatose state.

I look up at the bedazzled sky. Never have I seen so many stars, and the glorious moon looks different from the moon above Times Square in New York and especially different from the moon above my grandparents' cottage that night in November as I stood with my mother, aching to hear the silent sea.

When I walk back to our private log cabin at the Cody ranch, I climb into bed with my journal. I've made a list of questions for the Universe, and I decide I finally know the answer to one of them.

Questions for the Universe

1. Where is he? You know, my dance partner.
2. Am I ever going to have children?
3. What is my purpose on this planet?
4. Am I on the right path?
5. Why was I born a woman? Was I ever a man in a past life?
6. Where is my missing black wool sock?
7. If Anne Frank had escaped the gestapo, what other books would she have written?
8. Why did I dream about cash in a Bible in a hotel room and then walk into the Garden of Gethsemane? Why are my dreams so vivid?
9. Why do some people suffer, while others are blissful?
10. Am I asking the right questions?
11. Will we ever find a cure for cancer?
12. Will machines really take over the world?
13. What was Mona Lisa smiling about?
14. What did Granny Nora's spirit whisper to me after she died?
15. Why is there evil in the world?
16. Why are so many people sleepwalking through their lives?
17. Where do New Yorkers go when they die?
18. Why don't politicians support the arts, imagination, and education more?
19. Are our spirits on a journey through time and space?
20. Is the moon we see over the fields of Ireland on a cold November night indeed the same as the one we see over the blinding lights of Times Square?

No, Mom, it is not the same moon. Just as someone hears a song in a different color or smells a painting in a gallery with a different meaning, the moon, whether it's blue or pale, crescent or full, is never the same moon as viewed from Illinois to Istanbul, just as the pain I felt in losing my granny is not the same pain Luke feels in losing his grandmother. It's a shared experience through different heart monitors that interpret the world through different senses within each unique moment in time. It is a matter of perspective.

We rise before dawn to prepare for our early morning ride. After a hearty breakfast of eggs and bacon that I leave on my plate due to nerves, Lauren and I walk up a dirt lane that leads us to the horse corral. There, to our disappointment, we find Chase, the son of the Texan ranch owners. We should have expected Luke wouldn't make the last ride of the season, especially since he is leaving for the airport in a few hours.

Chase greets us with a warm smile. "Howdy!"

"Sorry to keep you waiting," I says. We were supposed to meet him at eight o'clock but got to chatting in the dining room with his mother, who was searching for allergy medication.

"I just have to warn you: I'm not only one hundred percent allergic to horses but also really nervous, so I need a very slow and boring horse, preferably ancient."

"Don't worry," Chase says. "I chose the slowest, oldest horse for you. My mother warned me in advance."

"Is it just a coincidence that the slowest, oldest horse is also the tallest?" I ask as Chase cups his hands for me to place a foot in order to throw my other leg over the saddle. I am regretting not using the yoga mat I brought with me. My body is stiff from sitting in the driver's seat each day.

Chase attends to Lauren, when I make another observation.

"Is it also a coincidence that my horse is black, and Lauren's is reddish brown?" I notice our horses' manes match our own.

He smiles at me as he tightens Lauren's saddle. "That was intentional."

I am beginning to like this married cowboy just as much as our single one. They sure make them all easy on the eyes down south.

"By the way, your horse's name is Tequila, and Lauren's over here is called Kahlúa," he says as he mounts his horse.

"I hope they didn't toast to their namesake this morning." Lauren laughs, patting her horse tenderly.

After giving a few tips on how to make our new mode of transportation stop and go, Chase leads us on a two-hour ride into the Shoshone National Forest, where we cross over loose rocks in tiny brooks and climb steep terrain through a dense wooded trail under the brilliant autumn sun. I wish I had brought my gloves and worn another layer when we ride through the shaded areas. At least I wore my leather cowgirl hat I purchased in Argentina. I am missing only the proper boots.

At one point, Chase notices my saddle is coming loose, so he parks his horse at a nearby tree and tightens my straps. That's when I see a gun secured in his belt.

"Is that gun for show or safety, or do you plan on shooting us during the ride if we get out of line?" I ask, looking at his weapon.

He laughs. "I carry it just in case we come across a bear or coyote." His tone is calm and confident. I tell myself not to panic as my eyes scan the shadows under the nearby trees.

Aunt Peg calls daily, asking us to avoid Yellowstone, as a few people have been attacked by bears in recent weeks, but I can't avoid Yellowstone. That was Granny's favorite part of the trip. She spent two whole weeks in that park.

Chase leads us up a narrow trail that plunges into an abyss of the tops of pine trees until we reach a peak that overlooks miles of jagged rock and majestic landscape. We pause there to take in the scene. It is nine o'clock, the time I was usually climbing up the escalator in the subway station on my way to work. Now here I am, on a horse, at the top of a hill, overlooking the grandness of the American wilderness beside a polite twenty-two-year-old cowboy whose dream is to open an orphanage with his young wife in a needy country somewhere in the world. He explained on our quiet ride through the tranquil forest that he and his bride have traveled extensively and were devastated by the conditions they witnessed in parts of Africa, among other places. I gained a new respect for his parents, who raised a selfless young man.

Your worth is determined by your service to others.

As we trot back toward the ranch, we pause so Chase can cut a sprig of sage for each of us to inhale, and suddenly, we see a figure up on a hill, illuminated by the bright morning sun. It looks like a bare-chested man on a horse, wearing feathered headgear. He sits regally on the animal.

Lauren gasps. "Wait—is that a Native American?"

Chase looks up as we pull the reins on our horses to stop. The figure slowly rides down the hill as Lauren and I scramble to find our cameras. As the figure comes closer, Chase begins to laugh. It is Luke, dressed up like a Native American. He planned to wear the headgear for tours with children during the summer, but he never got the chance, so on this last day in Wyoming, he decided to adorn himself with traditional ceremonial headgear and fool us into thinking he was the real deal. It was a playful trick, and we all share a good laugh. It is good to hear him laugh. Lauren and I feel special that he would make the effort even though his flight leaves in a few short hours to bring him to his grandmother's funeral.

Back at the ranch, the Texan family is packed and ready to drive south for the winter, just like the butterflies. This is a ritual they perform each year, closing down the ranch for the season—but not before they each sit at the wheel of our Silverado and take numerous photos outside the main cabin with Luke, Lorna, and the rest of the gang. We are included in all of their photographs. They even include the little red toy model Bel Air that Ted gave me in Ohio at the Duramax plant. Bill, Chase's father, who eerily resembles George Bush in both his accent and facial expressions, gets a kick out of how the toy model looks real in photographs if they're taken from the right angle. He lies on the dirt pavement to the amusement of his family as he takes pictures of my toy car with my camera, laughing so hard he can barely keep steady. As her husband lies on the ground, Trish hands us a gift bag containing two large coffee mugs she saw us admiring in the gift shop in their lobby. She also gives us prepaid passes to enter Yellowstone. I already have given them all copies of my CDs and Chevy memorabilia. I didn't expect gifts in return.

After we finally climb into our Silverado and drive down their long driveway to the main road, we stop at the gate so Chase can jump out of his father's vehicle and close it behind us. The gifts, embraces, tears, and dirt road all remind me of the ritual when I said farewell to my grandparents each summer. These strangers feel like family, and I don't want to leave them just yet. We only spent one night in their home, in their dining room, at their fire pit, and under their stars, but we bonded like long-lost cousins, and we part as friends.

I honk as we pause at the entrance to the main road, and they open their windows.

"Bye, y'all!" I call to them, and the family laughs heartily at my attempt at a Texan drawl, waving to us as we drive in opposite directions.

I catch a glimpse of Luke in the backseat, and a line from a poem by Emily Dickinson enters my mind: "Because I could not stop for death, he kindly stopped for me." Funerals put everything in perspective.

23

Don't Fence Me In—Roy Rogers

One o'clock in the afternoon is a bit late in the day to be entering a national park as large and as grand as Yellowstone, especially since we are only going to spend a few hours driving through it rather than camping out for two weeks, as my family did, but we have finally released the pace of New York from our systems—I believe our time spent on the ranch helped us do that—so we had no desire to race to get to the park after our early morning horse ride.

Often, when I arrive at Dublin Airport, I spit out an itinerary as my uncle Manus drives me to his house for the night before we head up to the farm in Donegal.

"Tara," he tells me, "you're in Ireland now, so take off your watch, and enjoy the scenery."

It's tragic that we New Yorkers need to be told that, but it does take a good week or so to settle into the rhythm of a place that abides by a slower pace.

And Yellowstone does abide by its own pace. Traffic often slows down to a halt when a herd of buffalo—or American bison, as they are officially called—are grazing in the alpine meadows or prairies. Tourists get dangerously close to the herd, not realizing the massive mammals will attack if provoked and can outrun a human at up to forty miles per hour despite their lethargic appearance during feeding time. There are two herds in Yellowstone, which make up approximately 3,700 bison. Lauren thinks that is a large number, but I read in our brochures that there were actually about sixty million in North America before they were almost hunted to extinction by the 1880s. I saw a few of their hunted heads above the fireplace in President Teddy Roosevelt's home at Sagamore Hill in Oyster Bay, New York. As we lean out of the car and up through the sunroof of the Silverado to take photos of these giant creatures having their lunch, I can't help but think of Marie Antoinette and her young king Louis, who sat on display in court as they ate in front of an assembly line of curious onlookers.

We encounter more than one rogue bison walking along the main road throughout the afternoon. Bison generally tend to stay in herds, so we are warned to keep clear of the massive males who walk to the beat of their own drum. We feel somewhat safe while driving alongside them in our equally massive truck, but I don't want to tempt fate.

One lone bison walks alongside our vehicle, never faltering in his slow but steady pace. *Poor old lonely fellow. No friends, no family, no Saturday night date, and here it being mating season.* I feel for the guy. It's a curse to be alone in a place with such generous amounts of geothermal activity. He could be hooking up with the ladies in the hot tubs near all the geysers. I know his pain. He isn't suffering from a mental disorder. He is just tired of the same old prairie grass and needs a change of scenery and a new menu. American bison are naturally a migratory bunch. This loner is breaking out on his own road trip. I wish I could have warned him as we drive off and leave him there making his way north that once he leaves the perimeter of the park, those cowboys in Montana have the right to shoot to kill if he gets too close to Main Street. And I thought I had it bad living near the Boulevard of Death.

As I have learned recently in witnessing roosters, raccoons, and the mass migration of butterflies, when animals cross our path with purpose or stand out to make sure we take notice, they have a message to share. According to Native Americans, buffalo represent a sacred life and abundance. A buffalo symbolizes the strength to overcome difficulties. Its presence lets us know we are on the right path and that something good is about to happen in our future. It wants us to express our gratitude to the Universe for all the blessings in our lives. Its presence makes us feel safe because it protects its own family, and seeing a buffalo may indicate we are being protected by the spirits of our ancestors.

When Granny Catherine was in Yellowstone, she finally called home from a pay phone to tell my granddad where they were. It was the first call she'd made since the day they left. Granddad was frantic. Father Peter had called New York numerous times from Spokane. On the first call, he wondered if they had even left home yet. They had been on the road for a month. They should have reached Washington already, my granddad replied to his worried brother. Had they gotten lost? Had they been in an accident? But Granny told him to calm his nerves. They were having a ball and were staying in the park as long as they didn't get attacked by a bear, as they often heard the grizzlies poking around outside their tent and car at night, looking for leftovers. That bit of news didn't ease his concerns.

Lauren and I pull over when we see the phone booth, and I make that symbolic phone call home. I make a collect call to my parents' landline, but they don't answer. I keep forgetting about the time difference.

One night in Yellowstone, Granny was surprised to bump into a family she'd met at a campsite back in Wisconsin in the early part of their journey. The family was driving to Alaska from their home in Florida. While in Wisconsin, they'd suggested Granny take a detour and go see the Dickeyville Grotto on the grounds of the Holy Ghost Parish, so she had. It was a shrine built by a Catholic priest out of respect for God and country using stones, seashells, cut glass, gems, pottery, sea urchins, amber, petrified wood, starfish, coal, and even fool's gold. She was up for any suggestions from fellow trekkers. When she bumped into the family again in Yellowstone a few weeks later, she was surprised to see their familiar faces. On another night, as both families toasted marshmallows over the fire, she asked their father, "Aren't you afraid of getting lost driving such a long distance?" I don't think she realized she was driving a similar distance.

The father responded, "How can you get lost when you haven't left the planet?" According to my aunt Peg, his comment made a great impression on her mother.

As the sun begins to set, I suggest to Lauren that we exit the park and find a place to stay somewhere in Montana for the night. We are too far from Old Faithful to take a look at the most famous site in the park, but we are satisfied with our visit to the Grand Canyon of Yellowstone, a large canyon twenty-four miles long on the Yellowstone River, where we first heard the dull roaring sound of the falls before our eyes came upon the beautiful site. I stood at Inspiration Point and looked down in amazement, wondering what it had been like for the first explorers to come upon such a scene. Lauren and I didn't speak as we stared down at the roaring river below as it carved its way through the canyon, which looked like a painting through my lens. I experienced a moment of intense emotion as I imagined Granny Catherine standing on that very spot, seeing the site as if through her eyes.

Where are you taking me?

Upon exiting the northern gate, we encounter a herd of elk that brings traffic to a standstill. The males, with their large antlers, are impressive—much more impressive than the traffic jams caused by taxis and delivery trucks. The elk is considered one of the most powerful spirit animals. When elks cross your path, the Universe is telling you that success is coming in your future, but you must be patient. In the meantime, maintain good relationships with family and friends, and build your community.

As the sun sets behind the purple mountains of Montana, I hear the wind call my name. "She's coming," it says to the night. "She has arrived."

24

Synchronicity—The Police

Perhaps it was the backdrop of a gorgeous landscape that rivaled the beauty and brawn of Brad Pitt in the film *A River Runs through It* that drew me to Big Sky Country, whose state tree is the Ponderosa pine. Granny was wooed by Montana on the big screen as well, with pictures like 1954's *Cattle Queen of Montana*, starring Ronald Reagan and Barbara Stanwyck. Stanwyck played a daring flame-haired woman nicknamed Sierra Nevada by her Native American neighbors. No wonder Granny was enchanted by the Wild West after watching movie trailers of independent redheaded women like herself riding horses, shooting guns, and defending cattle in glorious Technicolor, all with a dramatic soundtrack.

Or perhaps the ghosts of my ancestors were calling me to the mountainous state. I remember hearing over the years that Butte, Montana, is an Irish town, perhaps more Irish than New York, Chicago, or Boston claims to be. I have to see it to believe it.

When Granny Catherine arrived in Butte, she stayed in the Towey Hotel, which was owned by another independent gal named Bessie Towey. Bessie was a neighbor of my grandfather's back in Ireland. She inherited the hotel from her father and boarded ninety miners at a time, all Irish. Men occupied the beds in eight-hour shifts and shared a single toilet. Bessie managed the hotel alone until she decided to marry one of those miners to assist her in her later years. She once let Louis Armstrong stay in her hotel when he was performing and touring out west because no other hotel would admit a person of color at the time.

Before I left on my road trip, I researched the Towey Hotel because I wanted to see if I could stay in at least one hotel that I knew for sure my granny had stayed in, as I knew it still existed. However, I found out it no longer operated as a hotel. A website mentioned that it was an antique store, so I thought perhaps Lauren and I could go inside to take a few photos.

We drive into Butte, and I feel as if I have stepped back in time. The buildings haven't changed in well over a century. We park in the center of Uptown and walk a few blocks, searching for the old hotel, as abandoned storefronts whisper to us in the wind. When we find the hotel, we are disappointed to see its storefront darkened. It is obviously no longer an antique shop. But there is something I must discover behind its door. I squint and look up at the sign, which still reads, "Towey Hotel."

I decide to inquire at a nearby grocery. A friendly looking woman stands behind the counter at the Dancing Rainbow Natural Grocery.

"Hi. I'm curious to know about the abandoned hotel next door," I say as the woman greets me with a kind smile.

"Oh, that's not abandoned. A couple live there now, it's a private residence." She sorts items as she speaks.

"The reason I ask is because my Irish grandmother stayed there in 1957."

The woman stops her sorting. "Well, then she must have known Bessie."

"Yes! They were great friends. That's why my granny came to Butte on her way to Spokane."

"My goodness. I'm Jude." She extends her hand.

"I'm Tara, and this is Lauren." I look back at the sign with the rainbow over the shop's entrance and make an interesting connection in my mind. I think about Judy Garland's voice singing "Over the Rainbow." I think about Professor Pete in front of the yellow Corn Palace, reminiscing about seeing *Wicked* ten times on Broadway. I think about Dr. Christine, the Barry Manilow backup singer whom I called Glinda the Good Witch after she hypnotized me on her couch on the Upper West Side of Manhattan. I think about Toto, the Spanish ice sculptor who had a near-death experience. I think about my dancing friend, Fayth, in Chicago, whose fiancé, Jordan, is from Kansas. I think about Dorothy, who made her Free Ice Water sign in 1931 in Wall, South Dakota. I think about the one pair of red high heels I packed, which I have yet to wear during my road trip. The Universe is speaking to me through the symbols of a 1939 Hollywood musical.

"Welcome to Butte!" Jude exclaims. "I was very close to Bessie Towey. In fact, I was with her the day she died." She reaches up behind the counter and takes a large frame off the wall. "I took these pictures from her apartment after she passed. I didn't want anyone to throw them away, and I put this together for her memorial," she says, fingering the collage of images of Bessie in the 1940s. Bessie is walking down the main street, looking like a Hollywood starlet in her sunglasses and wide-legged trousers.

"Lauren, look at this!" I call to my copilot, who has been examining the health food.

"February 9, 1902, to July 2, 1996. Wow, she was gorgeous! And a good age." Lauren examines the images of Bessie's cottage in Ireland, her wedding day to the miner Mr. Mulhern, and the couple standing outside the hotel.

"She must have been some tough cookie, managing a hotel with all those men under her feet," I say, looking at her strong shoulders and arms, which appear to have had purpose.

"Oh, she was sharp—let me tell you. And what a sense of humor! I just miss her so much." Jude holds the frame in her hands one more time before she returns it to its place on the wall behind the counter. "Do you want to meet the couple who own the place now?"

"Of course!"

"I think they went out for the day, but they are a friendly couple, and I'm sure they'll give you a tour. Gimme your phone number, and I'll let you know." Jude hands me a pen and paper.

As I write down my number, Lauren brings a couple chocolate bars to the counter, one for me and one for her. Only we would enter a health-food store and walk out with candy.

"I also have an audio recording of Bessie that they used for the historical archives in town. I can make you a copy if you'd like. How long are you staying?" Jude puts my number in a safe place behind the counter.

"Oh, we leave in the morning." I sigh, disappointed we can't remain in this town that has ghost stories ready to be revealed in the rafters.

"Well, come back on your way out of town, and I'll have it ready for you." She waves to us as we exit the store and make our way across the street to another shop with an enticing name.

Cavanagh's County Celtic wears an emerald-and-gold sign above its door. I tell Lauren I want to get a souvenir that says something about the Irish in Butte. As we enter the store, the dominant color green makes me wonder if this is indeed the Emerald City in the Land of Oz. The interior looks like the duty-free shops at Shannon Airport, with its green, white, and gold T-shirts; shamrock-covered teapots; Irish music CDs; and boxes of Barry's Tea, in addition to a large supply of Irish chocolates and biscuits. Lauren regrets buying the organic chocolate in the grocery store.

The woman behind the counter eyes us from the moment we enter the shop, despite the number of other customers milling about. When I approach the counter to look through a bowl of shamrock pins, she begins her inquiry.

"Where are you from?"

"New York."

"You look like you just arrived from Ireland. What about your redheaded companion there?"

"She's more American than I am. My mother and grandparents are from Ireland."

"What brings you to Butte?"

"My granny from Waterford stayed here in the Towey Hotel across the street in 1957. I'm on a quest. Do you mind if I ask you some questions?"

She looks at me as a New Yorker would, guarded and trying to figure me out. I see an Irish music CD on her counter. It's the one playing on the loudspeaker in the shop.

"Here." I reach into my purse. "Everyone I interview gets a free CD." I hand her my *Black Irish* CD. Her face lights up.

"You're a musician? Oh, we have to put this on." She hands the CD to her assistant and asks that she play track number two, "Danny Boy." As soon as my voice fills the cluttered shop, the other customers come to the counter.

"Is that CD for sale?"

"Is that you?"

"Can I buy a copy? No, make that two copies."

Lauren has to make two trips to the truck to get more CDs. I walked into the shop with the intention of buying a single souvenir, and I will walk out with two complimentary hunter-green Butte T-shirts as well as more than one hundred dollars' worth of CD sales. Monica, the owner, holds our attention for more than two hours, chatting about Ireland, music, and the annual An Ri Ra Irish festival the city hosts every August, when they fly in traditional Irish bands to perform.

"You should come back for that. You could even perform with your band." She gives us each a warm hug and walks us to the door with our bag of souvenirs. I know I have to come back, especially since we have spent the entire afternoon in the historic town and only entered two establishments, a grocery store and a Celtic gift shop. There is much more to uncover, but as usual, we are running out of time, and we have to eat dinner before heading back to our hotel for the night.

We are staying in room 308 at the historic Finlen, a grand hotel on Broadway designed after the Hotel Astor in New York.

Presidents Roosevelt, Truman, and Kennedy all stayed at the Finlen, so I suppose it will do.

Jude calls us from her store at eight in the morning. She has Bessie Towey's audio interview copied for us and says the friendly couple are out for their morning walk, but they'll be happy to let us in and show us around when they return.

She meets us in front of the old hotel and rings the bell, and we wait for Paul and Allison to come downstairs. The first thing we notice after their friendly reception at the door is a framed poster on the gold wallpaper in the stairwell. The image is of a monarch butterfly, and the caption reads, "No One Is Free When Others Are Oppressed." When we climb to the top of the stairs, I ask if the wallpaper is the original.

"We haven't changed a thing since Bessie lived here," Paul tells us. "All the fixtures, moldings, and tiles and even the kitchen stove and cabinets are all original."

"May I take photos?" Lauren asks.

"Oh, be our guest." Allison leads Lauren down the long, narrow hall of the old hotel.

"We use the front rooms mostly." Paul leads us on a tour as he turns lights on in each room we enter. "But we've maintained a few of the guest rooms for when friends visit. You gals could have stayed here if we'd known you were in town."

Lauren and I look at each other. If only we could have arranged that. But as I wander through the old building, I begin to think I might not have liked staying here at night.

"Is this place haunted?" I ask, peering down the remainder of the long hallway, which Paul chooses not to illuminate. I can sense a presence.

"Oh, I would say so, yes. There are all kinds of things that go bump in the night in this building and in a number of historic buildings in town. Butte is the largest historic district in the entire country because not much has been torn down or modernized."

I peek into the one and only water closet the ninety miners shared. I can't imagine Bessie having the task of cleaning that toilet.

We move into the brightly lit front room overlooking the street below. My eyes devour the floral-print wallpaper and the plants sitting casually in a white sink attached to the wall. I noticed there's one in each guest room. My granny stayed in this hotel. My father and aunt ate in that kitchen. Their eyes saw exactly what I am seeing. There are even photographs of Bessie on the wall. Nothing has been changed. This is a gift.

"I always felt this desire or need to come to Montana," I tell our hosts as I walk around their front room, examining the furniture. "I never knew why. But I'm discovering connections here, and my grannies keep making their presence known to me in so many ways. I never knew my dad's mother, and suddenly, I know so much about her. I suppose all I had to do was ask." I touch the doorknob of the sitting room and imagine my grandmother's fingers wrapping around it. The fingerprints might have been wiped away, but I can sense her strong grip.

"There's something magical about Butte." Paul is leaning against a wall, watching Lauren take photos of the artifacts in the room. "We felt it when we drove through here on vacation. It called to us. There was something in the air. We knew we had to live here. We sold our place in Colorado and moved here as fast as we could."

I understand what he is talking about. I feel it too.

When we finally walk down to the street to say farewell, I point to the address of the Towey Hotel. "Eleven?"

"Oh, that's a significant number," Allison says as she touches my arm.

"I know. It's a number that keeps coming up for me. I notice it because it's the day I was born, April 11. And every time I look at a clock, it reads 11:11 or 4:11 or 9:11." I shield the sun from my eyes as I look up at their address.

"It's a master number of the Universe that symbolizes new beginnings or transformation," Allison says.

Paul lowers his voice as if it's a secret. "The district we are standing in is the eleventh. So when we saw the hotel address, we knew we had to purchase it. What was your hotel number at the Finlen?"

"It was 308," Lauren says.

"Three plus eight. That adds up to eleven!" Paul exclaims.

"Oh my God," Lauren says. She and I look at each other.

"And what is today's date?" Paul asks us.

We have to think. "The twenty-ninth," Lauren says, looking at her phone.

"Holy cannoli, that adds up to eleven too!" I am amazed by the connections. "Hey! We're on this Chevy road trip, and Chevrolet began one hundred years ago, in 1911!"

"Paul and I are really into numerology. The number eleven also represents balance and fulfillment." Allison's voice seems far away. "If that number keeps coming up for you, it might be the Universe sending you a magical message asking if you are ready to awaken to your higher consciousness and remember your soul's purpose. You must have a very intuitive soul, especially if you receive so many messages from your grannies."

We all examine each other's faces and reflect on her words.

"November 11, 2011, is approaching next month, the eleventh day of the eleventh month of the eleventh year in the century," I say.

"Oh my, I didn't even realize. You should do something really significant on that date," Allison says, and Paul nods in agreement.

After a bunch of warm wishes, hugs, and kisses, we leave Butte, and as Lauren drives the Silverado, on my smartphone, I read interesting and eerie facts pertaining to the number eleven.

"The average adult male heart weighs eleven ounces. The first lunar landing was made by Apollo 11. King Tut's tomb had combinations of eleven in the jewelry he wore and had eleven oars surrounding his tomb. The number of guns in a gun salute of the US Army, Air Force, and Marine Corps is eleven. After Judas was disgraced in the Garden of Gethsemane, the remaining apostles of

Jesus were described as the Eleven. World War I ended on November 11, the eleventh hour of the eleventh day of the eleventh month, and the first plane that hit the World Trade Center on September 11 in New York, which happens to be the eleventh state of the union, was Flight 11, which had eleven crew members."

"It's a master number that symbolizes new beginnings," Allison had told us. "The Universe is asking you to awaken."

Everything seems to add up to eleven. My mother was handed ninety-two dollars collected by her aunts and uncles when she arrived at the dock in New York Harbor. She arrived in November, the eleventh month, of the year 1957, whose numbers add up to twenty-two, of which the number eleven is the root. Her young neighbor in New York counted ninety-two roosters in Mom's house, where she resurrected the symbol after Granny Nora killed her rooster in Donegal. While Granddad was dying of pancreatic cancer in Ireland, Mom and I visited Anne Frank's hiding place in Amsterdam, located at 263 Prinsengracht Street, where a memoir was written that inspired the world. The number of people who lived in Wall, South Dakota, when Dorothy made her Free Ice Water sign was 326.

Then there are the dates. I was born on April 11. My first kiss was November 11. My young mother wrote a letter to her parents from the boat as she crossed the Atlantic and dated it November 11. I traveled to London to fulfill Granny Nora's last wish on November 11, and Granny Catherine was born in November. The monarch butterflies arrive in Mexico after their migration on November 1, the Day of the Dead. I'm on a symbolic journey in the year 2011, and I'm being sponsored by Chevrolet, which began making cars in 1911.

Tell me that isn't synchronicity! Tell me that isn't the Universe shouting, "Wake up!" to the bread crumbs and cosmic connections it has carefully, intentionally, and purposefully placed before me. Some might say it's just a coincidence, but I am starting to realize the Universe is full of magical and mystical signs, and nothing is a coincidence.

25

Earth Angel—The Penguins

They only had thirty-eight more minutes to drive before they reached their destination of Spokane, Washington, where my granduncle Father Peter waited patiently. However, as they drove through Idaho, Granny Catherine noticed a luminous lake shimmering on the edge of the resort town of Coeur d'Alene. The water looked inviting, and as it was a hot day in August, they decided to get milkshakes and then go for a swim.

As Lauren and I drive through the lake city named by French Canadian fur traders, we realize why some folks call it a little slice of heaven. It looks as if a Swiss Alpine village married a Miami Beach resort, with a glacier-gouged lake surrounded by forest-covered mountains on one side and beachfront property with shake shacks and margaritas on the other side.

We drive within sight of the lake, searching for a place to buy our milkshakes. It was Granny's first time drinking the thick, cold, creamy substance. We assume she bought her milkshake along the lake, at a diner or shop within walking distance.

"That's it!" I shout at Lauren, who sits in the passenger seat, scanning the sidewalk.

"What? Where?"

"Paul Bunyan!"

"Who?"

"Look!"

I pull into a drive-in on Northwest Boulevard where the

larger-than-life giant lumberjack stands holding his ax. The Paul Bunyan drive-through and sit-in diner looks at least fifty years old. The girl inside the window confirms that it is indeed one of the oldest burger joints in town and has been in the same spot since the early 1950s. They had to demolish the original building a little more than ten years ago because it was pretty run down; however, nothing about the new edifice looks modern, especially big old Paul Bunyan standing over the boulevard. It looks as if it could be the original sign that welcomed drivers, such as my granny. Even if it's not where she had her first milkshake, it sure feels like it.

I try to imagine the classic cars lined up at the drive-through window with customers waiting to order their corn dogs, vanilla Cokes, Blue Ox burgers, and Hammy Whammys (layers of thin fried ham and yellow mustard on a double-sized roll). I order a chocolate shake, and Lauren asks for a malt. She jumps out of the truck to take photos of the counter girl handing me the shakes to document the symbolic deed.

When she gets back into the truck, we giggle in delight, and we cross the boulevard to head toward the parking lot beside the lake. Not twenty feet from the diner's curb, a '57 Chevy Bel Air pulls up alongside me.

"Oh my God! Oh my God!" I scream, and Lauren grabs my shake as I scramble to find my camera with my other hand still on to the steering wheel. I capture the car just before it pulls away.

"Did you get it?" Lauren is deliriously euphoric.

"Yes! Yes! Oh, I am lovin' this ride." I pass her the camera, as I need both hands to pull into the lot to park our monster truck.

"I can't believe we see one almost every day." Lauren shakes her head in amazement.

"Well, I think Granny Catherine was just letting us know we got the right shake shack."

We find a bench above the water's edge and sit in silence in the bright sun, sucking our thick shakes. A seaplane takes off from a nearby dock, and we watch it rise into the sky and disappear behind the Rocky Mountains.

As I gaze at the shimmering water, I imagine my dad and aunt jumping off the pier. They always had fun together. One morning, when Granny Catherine walked her oldest daughter, Cathleen, to Saint Margaret Mary's Elementary School in the Bronx, she returned to find her two younger children, Tommy and Peggy, had set fire to the apartment. They were playing cowboys and Indians. After Granny tore down the burning curtains, she chased after them with threatening words and the sting of her hand. "I'll lay you out in lavender!" she roared at them. I've never heard anyone say that expression before. It seems like such a lovely way to die, so fragrant and colorful.

Despite the trouble they often found themselves in, as they were little devils to the core, they had a lot of fun with their mother. She loved to dance and attended the Waterford Ball every November in New York—yes, in November. If Granddad was busy at work, she'd dress up her three children and take them to the ball, as she wouldn't miss it. On Sundays, she'd play Viennese waltzes on the record player after Mass, and they'd all dance in the living room, imagining they were at a grand ball in Vienna, just as I had experienced when I attended a ball in Vienna at the age of seventeen. On Halloween, she'd dress up like a ghost to scare the neighbors' children, roaring with laughter after seeing their frightful faces. She was rarely scared herself, only as a child in Waterford when the Protestant neighbor hosted fox hunts and led his horses racing down her lane past her parents' house. She'd hide in the kitchen with her pet pig, which was permitted to live in the house along with her kittens.

My aunt only saw her mother cry once, as they walked past the schoolyard filled with children in the Bronx. Granny Catherine stood at the fence and watched the strangers play as an empty bassinet sat at home with new baby clothes that were never worn by her daughter Monica Lewis.

Grief is yet another song the heart must sing to open the gate of all there is.

Otherwise, she was full of life, always up for taking the children to Radio City Music Hall, Saint Patrick's Cathedral on Fifth Avenue, the Museum of Natural History, the Bronx Zoo, or the beaches at Rockaway.

She loved going to the cinema, just as I do. The 1939 classic *Gone with the Wind* has always been my favorite film. It won the Oscar for Best Picture, beating the other popular film that year, *The Wizard of Oz*. My nickname in college was Scarlett because I resemble the main character, with her green eyes, pale skin, and dark hair. Americans assume I was named Tara after the Georgian plantation in the movie. When I asked Aunt Cathleen what her mother's favorite film was, I almost couldn't believe it was the same as mine, *Gone with the Wind*. I have much in common with this flame-haired woman I never met.

I look over at my ginger-haired companion, who has been quietly struggling with her thick malt, and motion that we should move toward the water. We roll up our jeans, take off our shoes, and plunge our pale feet with matching red pedicures into the cold lake. We aren't about to perform full-bodied swan dives since it is a day shy of October, but for symbolic reasons, I know I have to christen my toes. After the initial shock, we get used to the temperature and linger a few moments longer before we get back in the truck. I turn on the satellite radio as we pull out of the parking lot and recognize the song.

"Hey! That's my dad's favorite song from when he was a teenager."

"What's the name of it?" she asks as she adjusts her sunglasses.

"'Earth Angel,'" I say, smiling, "by the Penguins."

"The Penguins? What kind of a band name is that?" She laughs.

"Lots of bands are named after birds," I inform her. "The Flamingos, the Eagles, the Byrds, Counting Crows, a Flock of Seagulls."

"That's interesting. I never thought about that. I wonder why bird names are so popular."

"Well, symbolically, birds represent freedom. They can reach the space between heaven and earth. Everyone wishes they could fly like a bird."

"But penguins don't fly," she says.

"True. However, they are really cool. They are always dressed to impress. They are sociable but monogamous. And they are amazing dads. Look at how the males protect the eggs while waiting for their partners to return to the community. They guard those eggs for months in the freezing snow and wind while the females are off hunting for food. Now, that is a modern-day couple."

Lauren sits quietly, listening to the song, for a few moments before she speaks. "I want to come back as a penguin when I die."

26

Faith—George Michael

Long-lost cousins are awaiting our arrival in Spokane, just as Father Peter O'Grady waited for Granny Catherine and my teenage father and aunt. Dottie and her adult daughter, Emily, have been in contact with me since I got on the road. Father Peter's mother shares their last name, so we have an ancestral connection. We met online a few years ago, when my family received an invitation to a reunion.

My copilot and I meet the luminous ladies in the morning after breakfast, and they agree to take us from our hotel to Saint Aloysius, where Father Peter worked. My goal is to visit the church where he preached and taught on the Gonzaga University campus and then visit his tombstone. I have no idea what to expect. Apparently, Father Peter's spirit is about to pull out the red carpet for us.

Dottie and Emily are a hoot from the moment we meet them. Dottie chooses to drive as her daughter sits in the backseat and swaps stories with my copilot. No matter the point at which we meet each other in our lives, my family members pick up where we left off. We must have all had a blast in our previous lives, because we can't help but finish each other's funny sentences. My friend Lauren is feeling like family every step of the way.

Dottie spent a number of years in Spokane after growing up in Butte, so she knows her way around. It is good to have a living guide at this point in our journey. She drives as close as she can to the campus, and as the four of us walk toward the church, we notice something extraordinary happening. Hundreds of children are assembling with their teachers, all wearing red, white, and blue.

"It's their hundredth anniversary!" I tell the ladies. "I read about this online when I was searching for someone who might have known my uncle."

"Did you know the celebration was happening today?" Emily asks, looking at all the preschoolers waddling behind their teachers.

"No, this is just pure coincidence," I say absentmindedly.

"Oh no, darlin', this ain't no coincidence." Dottie shakes her finger. "This here is Divine intervention."

My copilot and I laugh. I scan the growing crowd and search for a priest. There has to be someone here who knew my uncle. I watch as a young photographer climbs up a ladder with his zoom lens, preparing for the historic photograph of the schoolchildren on the steps of their church, Saint Aloysius, the patron saint of the youth. Then I spot a little man with a white collar. I approach the priest.

"Did you know Father Peter O'Grady?" I ask him.

"Ah, yes, I did," he says, keeping his eyes on the children.

"Really? Well, I'm his grandniece. I drove all the way from New York to come here." I am disappointed the priest does not appreciate the significance of my journey and mission. He appears not to care in the least, or perhaps he is too distracted because of the assembly and the schedule of events, with the photographer, the mass, and the celebration to follow. I take out a book of old photographs with pictures of Father Peter and my family. He glances at them with no comment, and his eyes move elsewhere.

Suddenly, a tall balding man standing nearby approaches me.

"Did you say you are related to Father O'Grady?" His eyes are kind.

"Yes! He was my father's favorite uncle. I just drove across country to come here."

"You came for the anniversary?" The man with the kind eyes is surprised.

"No, I just happened to come upon this scene today. I only came to see the church and to go to his tombstone."

"Well, that's just amazing. I'm Don." He extends his hand. "Father O'Grady was my Spanish teacher in high school."

"He taught Spanish?" I ask, stunned.

So that's why I always had an urge to study that language. I began my study of Spanish in high school, and then I lived in Seville, Spain, and Buenos Aires, Argentina, to keep practicing the language. It's all coming together.

"He was one of my favorite teachers of all time. What a great man. Can I see those photographs you have there?" He leans into my book, examining every image with extreme attention.

I look around for Lauren and my cousins, but they have gone inside the church to take photos. The photographer on the ladder is trying to get the attention of the hundreds of children on the steps of the church. He explains to them through a megaphone that when he counts to three, they should all shout, "Go Zags!" in unison.

One young boy shouts back, "What if I don't like the Zags?" The crowd of parents standing on the sidelines laughs.

"Do you know where the cemetery is located—the one Father Peter is buried in?" I ask Don.

"Oh sure, that's in Mount Saint Michael's. Would you like me to take you there?"

"Would I? Oh, this day just keeps getting better. Let me find the girls."

I run inside the empty church to find Lauren taking pictures around the scaffolding. Saint Al's is apparently getting a facelift in its hundredth year. I am lucky to have a friend who is also a photographer, as she is documenting every inch of my historic family road trip.

I walk down the aisle to the left of the altar to light a candle. Lauren discreetly captures the moment like a wedding photographer who doesn't want to get in between the newlywed couple and the Holy Spirit. I whisper a prayer for Granny Catherine and for Father

Peter, thanking both of them for leading me here to this place. I haven't set foot in a church in ages.

I was a religious child. How could I not have been, with a mother named Mary and a carpenter for a father? Dad even built a go-cart made from the wood scraps of pews in our local church when it was going through renovations. All the kids on the block wanted a ride. My brother and I called ourselves the Holy Rollers.

I attended Catholic schools from third grade through my master's degree in graduate school. That's sixteen years of religious education. But I stopped going to Mass because I had doubts. The stories we were taught didn't make sense, and the priests scolded us each week, talking about how guilty and sinful we all were. My mother said she used to like going to church when the mass was spoken in Latin, but now that it's in English, there's no mystery, she says, and the mystery is what made it all the more alluring to her. But I don't want mystery. I want truth. And I don't want to be scolded.

My favorite part of the mass was when we would shake hands with the people around us to share a sign of peace. I always felt a surge of energy when I looked into the other parishioners' eyes and touched their hands. There was healing in those hands. The sense of community in that gesture was electrifying. But my mother warned me that shaking people's hands helped spread cold and flu viruses, and I became a germophobe, so I avoided the ceremony altogether. My relationship with the church and everything I was raised to believe slipped into the background of my daily rituals like a fuzzy channel between stations on a wireless radio.

I began to stay outside and sit under an oak tree to reflect, meditate, and pray in my own way, listening to the robins sing and watching the sky change colors, because I understand God mostly when encountering nature. I never lost faith in the sacredness of life or the idea that there is indeed a great force in the Universe that connects all of us. I knew my soul needed to find the right channel to tune in to but on my terms, without guilt and without blind devotion.

I look up at the pulpit in Saint Aloysius and imagine my father's uncle giving a humorous homily. He was the most gorgeous priest I ever saw, with his black curls and a twinkle in his eye. All the women in the parish fancied him. They couldn't resist his charming personality, Irish accent and all. According to my father, he was not only a great musician but also an extraordinary athlete. Some say he could have been a professional baseball player if he hadn't answered God's call. He was an all-around swell character.

It's a shame he was stationed so far from us. The Jesuits sent him first to Wyoming, then to Idaho, and finally to Washington. He occasionally came to New York, and I remember visiting him once in Boise when I was ten years old. He made me believe he was in charge of picking those famous Idaho potatoes we bought in our local grocery back in Queens, because at the time, there was a brand of potato chips called O'Grady's. I would have believed anything he told me.

Father Peter's former student Don informs me that he is a retired detective. Dottie follows his car. I call my dad to let him know we are getting a police escort to Father Peter's grave. He can't believe it. Then I scream into the phone, and Dottie swerves her car in fright.

"What is it?" she asks, worried I have bad news.

I throw the phone into the backseat, and my copilot, Lauren, catches it. She knows why I am screaming.

"Hello? Tom?" She immediately picks up the conversation with my father. "This is Lauren. Hi. Yeah, sorry about that. Tara just saw another '57 Chevy Bel Air, so she had to grab her camera," she tells my father, who is no doubt just as worried as our driver.

"And it's red!" I shout at the backseat.

"It's a red one," she says to my dad. "We keep seeing either red or black—every color, really. Yeah, it's amazing. Okay, here's Tara again." She hands the phone back to me after I've snapped the shot.

"Oh, Dad, I wish you were here, especially today."

I can hear him getting choked up on the phone before he answers that he wishes he were here too. He often sees a red cardinal in his backyard when he's drinking his morning coffee. I read somewhere that cardinals are the reincarnated spirits of the clergy, so my dad understands the symbolism of that Bel Air being red. He too believes in signs.

We follow Detective Don up a steep hill to a cemetery overlooking all of Spokane. It is a quiet, grassy corner of the world under a few friendly trees, a lovely place to rest eternally. We walk across the dew-covered grass to a sign listing all the names of the men buried on the hill.

Emily reads them out loud, searching for my uncle's plot. "Maguire, Mahoney, Maloney, McCulloch, McDermott, McDonald, McDonough, McMonagle, Monaghan, Nealen, O'Brien, O'Callaghan, O'Connor. O'Grady! Here we go. But there are so many more." She continues reading the Irish names. "O'Hara, O'Leary, O'Malley, O'Reilly, O'Sullivan. O'Boy!" She stops. "Section four, row ten!" she calls up to Don, who is in the area where the Jesuits are buried.

I notice that a water sprinkler is showering most of row ten. "I can't get close enough to take a photo without getting drenched," I say, realizing my father won't get to see the tombstone.

Then Don does something wonderful: he steps on the sprinkler in row eleven and stops the stream of water with his entire shoe.

"Now you can." He smiles as we all cheer.

I step up to the flat, simple stone. It is the only stone that has a bright pink flower beside it. I wonder who put it there. I read the dates to myself. He was born May 23, 1907, and died June 16, 1993. He was ordained as a priest on April 1, 1933—April Fools' Day. That makes sense, as he was quite the prankster. But what is this other date? November 11, 1939—another November 11. This specific date is significant to my family. It represents our new beginnings: a first kiss, a journey to a new land, and now a mysterious engraving on a tombstone, most likely honoring a date related to his service as a priest.

He was living in Spain at that time. That was where he studied to become a Jesuit priest, at the Irish College in the University of Salamanca during the 1930s—not the best time for a foreign priest to be in Spain. It was a chaotic environment with riots, strikes, and a depression. The government had lost control, and a civil war began in 1936. I heard a story from my dad that Father Peter had bullet shrapnel in his head due to confrontations between church and state during that period, but no more details were shared. Father Peter was mysterious in that way. Perhaps he felt there was no reason to focus on the negative—or the past.

My dad was inspired by the fragments of stories about his favorite uncle, who left Ireland to live and study in Spain in the 1930s. Dad made his way there thirty years later, in the 1960s, to explore the people, the language, and the land. Another thirty years later, in the 1990s, I landed on that same shore. At the time, I didn't know why I had the urge to fly to Spain, to live there and study the language and culture. I just knew I had to go, like the monarchs. Generation after generation, the butterflies fly to Mexico. They are led by instinct, just like my family, to Spanish-speaking counties. We are drawn like moths to the light.

Father Peter came to me in a dream recently. He sat before me, relaxed in his black suit and white collar, his hair still dark before he aged. He told me Granny Catherine is often in my parents' house, over my father's shoulder while he's washing dishes. That means she is always with us. He wanted me to know that. I had never dreamed of him before. It was nice to see his smile again.

When he used to visit New York, he told us jokes and played his flute in our living room. He even conducted Mass in our dining room one Sunday morning. I loved that he didn't ask me to change out of my pajamas, despite my mother's objections.

"Jesus won't mind. I put a good word in for you," he said, winking at me as he stuck out his tongue like a child.

"Father Peter sure had a sense of humor," Don says to me.

"What's that?" I look up from the tombstone.

"Only he would bring an Irish mist over his grave the very moment we came to visit." Don laughs as we all look around the graveyard. No other sprinkler is on, only the one Don is stopping with his now damp foot.

"Thanks for holding back the rain," I say to the kind detective, who waits for us to walk away before he releases his foot from the device.

Father Peter must have made these encounters happen with the cousins and Detective Don.

27

From Galway to Graceland— Richard Thompson

Seattle welcomes us with drizzle. It feels comforting to be on the edge of the pool of America again, away from the deep end in the middle, where the flatlands swallowed me up in the abyss of cornfields. I like being near the water. The sounds of the seagulls and the smell of the catch of the day are inviting. Even the rain. Of course, I can't imagine Seattle in sunshine. The sky is overcast the entire weekend, and the light drizzle introduces itself to my curls, making them exceptionally frizzy.

The smell of Pike Place Market reminds me of Killybegs, the fishing village about a half hour up the road from my Donegal granny's house, and the crowds packed five people deep in front of each vendor remind me of the subways in Times Square. It all feels familiar.

Lauren and I are spending the weekend with family. I have never met my cousin Kate. Her grandmother and my great-grandmother were sisters. Kate grew up on the East Coast, in upstate New York, but her husband's work took her across the country, and that's why I never knew she existed. Her mom is great friends with my aunt Peg back in New York, so they told me we had to meet up. As I mentioned, when I meet long-lost cousins, we just pick up where we left off. She makes us feel right at home in her big house just outside the city center.

When we arrive at the fish market, Kate introduces us to a friend standing behind a counter and throwing fish over onlookers into the arms of other fishmongers. It is an entertaining attraction, and it keeps my attention for a while, until Kate's husband suggests we eat at an Irish pub.

A large vase of purple hydrangeas greets us inside the cozy pub. It's my favorite flower. All flowers have had symbolic meanings throughout the ages. The hydrangea is a symbol of creating your own destiny, and numerologists have assigned it the number eleven, signifying mystical awareness. Yes, eleven. My granny Nora had loads of the blue and pink bushes with mophead flowers growing just outside her cottage door. Every time I see this flower, I think of her. She is always making her presence known to me. As I finger the petals, I recognize the song on the sound system.

"Listen!" I say to Lauren and Kate, who are getting the attention of the waitstaff. "It's 'From Galway to Graceland,' a song about a woman who leaves Ireland to visit the King at his tombstone in Memphis."

Lauren and Kate listen to the lyrics as we wait to be seated. It's a bit of a tragic comedy about an Irish woman who leaves her husband of twenty years to be with the deceased king of rock and roll. She's such an obsessed fan she has Elvis's name tattooed across her breast. The security guards handcuff the poor daft woman at closing time as she lies on his tombstone at Graceland. She believes she's married to Elvis. We all have our little fantasies. But maybe she was married to him in a past life. Perhaps they are soul mates. Anything is possible.

"It's amazing that his pelvis had the capacity to haunt women across the Atlantic," I say to no one in particular.

When my mother came to America in 1957, Elvis was at the height of his fame. She had already heard his music in Ireland. He was her soundtrack to the American dream. I remember the day he died. It was 1977. I was coloring with crayons, when I heard my mother cry. She was kneeling by the TV, wiping tears from her face. When I asked why she was so sad, she simply replied, "I loved him." I couldn't understand how my mommy could be in love with another man. His sideburns weren't as nice as Daddy's.

"You're very welcome!" An attractive woman greets us with an Irish accent. She has the look of Ireland in her eyes and on her purposeful hands, which have peeled their share of potatoes. There is authority in her stride as she directs us to a table in the back of the dimly lit pub. I sense she is the owner of the establishment.

It is the first Irish accent I have heard since I left New York. I can't determine exactly which county she is from, so I ask her.

"Northern Ireland," she answers. "Derry, to be exact," she proudly adds.

"When did you come to America?" I am curious to learn the details of her migration story.

"I left in the 1970s, during the troubles." She looks at the teenage faces of my cousin's daughters, knowing they have no idea what she is referring to. "Are you on yer holidays?" Irish are always good at making conversation.

"I'm on a mission from New York, but these are locals." I point to my family.

"My God, you look like yer off the boat with that face." She touches my bat-lightning hair.

"Wait till you hear her name," Lauren says.

"Tara O'Grady." I sit up straight.

"Tara O'Grady? Well, if that isn't Irish. And what age are ye?" She isn't shy in asking, and I'm not shy in revealing, until she tells me her intentions of marrying me off to her son, who is named after one of the leaders of the Dublin Easter Rising of 1916.

She suggests I order the smoked salmon and brie on Irish soda bread with a side of potato soup. After we eat, she leads me and the whole gang through a side door to the adjacent pub owned by her son.

"*Mo chrot!* This here is Tara. She's looking for a husband," the mother announces before she walks away to speak to a waiter and "attend to something at the bar."

The son and I turn the same color of scarlet. I am not even aware if we shake hands. He is as awkward as a polar bear on roller skates. I never asked the woman to play matchmaker. I try to make light of the moment.

"Does she always embarrass you like this?" I can't even look into his eyes.

"Yes," he answers, and then he excuses himself to "attend to something at the bar."

The mother returns to us eventually and escorts us to the front door when we say we have to leave. "Will ye not come back tonight to hear Luka Bloom perform?"

"*The* Luka Bloom, as in the brother of Christy Moore?" I am impressed.

"No, just some local fella." She waves her hand.

"Is he single? Are you trying to push him off on me as well?" I tease.

"Do you not fancy my son?" She wears her matchmaking face again.

"The question is, do you not fancy keeping him around?" I miss this sort of banter that the Irish are famous for.

"Och, well, time enough he should be married off and to a lovely girl such as yerself. Do you not wanna come in and have another look at him?" she asks, tugging at my raincoat. My cousins have already disappeared down the alley.

I give her a hug as I laugh into her shoulder. "No, but thank you. It was lovely to hear an Irish accent again."

As I walk down the lane, I call back to her, "And your potato soup was gorgeous!"

She smiles, waves, and continues to stand in the drizzle under the gray sky until I turn the corner and find my family.

"We thought you'd be engaged by now," Kate teases.

"Where to next?" I ask, trying to change the subject.

"Starbucks!"

When the Irish pub owner arrived to America in the 1970s,

Starbucks was also the new kid on the block. The international coffeehouse chain had opened a single narrow storefront in Seattle's historic Pike Place Market. In my opinion, drinking a pricey cup of joe does not evoke the romance of the high seas and seafaring tradition of the early coffee traders, as is intended by the company's name, which was inspired by Herman Melville's great American novel *Moby Dick*. Starbuck, a thoughtful and intellectual Quaker from Nantucket, was one of three mates on the ship chasing the great whale. Imagine what the author might think if he knew a character from his 1851 novel inspired the name of a coffee chain in almost twenty thousand stores in fifty-eight countries around the globe, from Galway to Graceland, especially since *Moby Dick* was a commercial failure when it was published.

28

Take Me Home, Country Roads—John Denver

I don't want to head back east. I don't want to return to routine, early morning commutes on crowded subways, and people who don't look me in the eye when I pass them on the street. I want to keep going and continue down through Oregon and California; across Nevada, Utah, and Colorado; down to New Mexico; across Texas, Louisiana, and Mississippi; on up to Tennessee, Kentucky, and West Virginia; back through Donegal, Pennsylvania, and New Jersey; and finally home to New York.

Even though the journey isn't over, it feels as if it is over. We have reached our destination, and now we have to backtrack pretty much the same route since we only have one week to cross the country on major highways and return the vehicles in Chicago and New York.

I decide to take a slight detour. Granny Catherine was so inspired by the open road in the summer of 1957 that she hit the road again the following summer of 1958, that time including her eldest daughter, Cathleen. They took a similar route but also made it to Nevada and California. They even explored Glacier National Park in Montana.

That's where I steer the Silverado after we say farewell to Kate and her family. Two and a half days is not enough time to share all our stories and songs. She cries as we pull out of her driveway in our truck packed with brownies and cookies she baked the night before our departure. If her husband had doused the car with holy water, it would have felt like my family ritual of leaving the Donegal farm, especially since Kate's dog chases our vehicle down the street as we disappear into the early morning fog.

Whitefish, Montana, is about a five-hour detour north off the main highway once we cross the state of Washington and pass Spokane. I am not just going there for the sake of seeing another national park, which is closed for the season anyway. I have one more long-lost relation to meet. My family discovered him online when he emailed my father.

He said his name was Bob Grady, and he was searching for relatives who had migrated from Ballaghaderreen, the town my father's father was from in Roscommon. Bob did not know of any other Grady relations in the United States. He wrote that he had gone to Ireland a few years before searching for his roots.

When I called Bob to tell him I was in the area, I let him know the name of the lodge we had booked for our one night in Whitefish. I figured we could meet him, have a meal, and then get back on our merry way. I'd always dreamed of staying in a lodge in Montana. I booked an affordable room in a building across from the main lodge overlooking the parking lot rather than the lake, but this gentleman, who was about the same age as my father, called me back to inform me that he had gone to the lodge and upgraded our room on his credit card. He figured if we were going so far out of our way to meet him, he wanted to do something for us.

A giant mounted bear greets us in the lobby, towering over a crackling fireplace. The bellboy leads us to our room, where we try to contain our enthusiasm until he is out of earshot. Talk about an upgrade! We have a kitchen with marble floors; a bathroom with a walk-in shower, a Jacuzzi, and two sinks; a living room area with a fireplace; teddy bears on our pillows; and a balcony overlooking the lake, marina, mountains, and, more importantly, swimming pool and hot tub.

Although it's October, Mother Nature is not aware of the season.

I packed my bags with wool sweaters from Donegal, expecting autumn in the mountains to be almost like winter, with snow and all, but I haven't worn one stitch of wool or fleece the entire trip. We are practically at the Canadian border, at the mouth of Glacier National Park, wearing our Chevy T-shirts without jackets.

"Want to explore the town?" Lauren asks, dancing around the suite like a kid in a candy shop.

"No way, Jose. We're putting on our bikinis and hitting that hot tub." I point at the pool and Jacuzzi below. "Besides, this upgrade is a gift. I want to enjoy every inch of this place and relax." Alabama Trevor's pause button is definitely being put to use tonight.

We make our way down to the empty patio by the pool and head straight to the hot tub. I still can't get over the fact that I am in my bathing suit in Montana in October. It makes me wonder if there are still glaciers in Glacier National Park.

The scenery is breathtaking. The sun is beginning to set behind the mountains. It casts a golden light on our faces as we watch birds fly close to the surface of the lake. I can almost hear their wings touch the water. Dad was right when he said to get off the beaten track and away from the main interstates.

Lauren and I stopped many times on our way to the lodge to take pictures of creeks and brooks that ran along the country roads, abandoned hundred-year-old shacks, isolated lakes, ancient rock formations, and autumn leaves on glorious trees sprouting out of the surrounding hills that became majestic purple mountains so close to heaven we could smell it. Our cameras couldn't capture the awe-inspiring scenery in all its glory. Our lenses weren't large enough. No lens is large enough. This is a sight to behold with the naked eye and experience with all the senses, not with technical devices.

I ease into the bubbling hot tub, and the soothing water caresses my skin, melting each muscle and bending each bone. I release a deep sigh and sink deeper into the healing waters. Lauren climbs in beside me and closes her eyes, making an audible sound of surrender.

Oh, majestic Montana, take me into your arms with your wide-open spaces, your big-sky splendor, and your wilderness that has been waiting for me to discover it. It has always been here waiting for me—the wind, the clouds, the birds, and the spirits of my ancestors. Here is my natural landscape, unspoiled by man for the sake of progress, where I can imagine, think, dream, reflect, and feed my spirit. I just had to get off the main highways, the congested, polluted roads full of distracting billboards and irritable drivers that keep us all from connecting to our core, to our spirit.

As I look out on the lake, the mountains, and the trees surrounding the oasis at my Montana lodge, I begin to understand the faith and devotion my Donegal grandparents practiced daily on their farm overlooking the rolling green hills and the ocean. Their skies provided rain, drenching their crops, which in turn fed their family with hearty potatoes from their fields, milk from their grass-fed cows, and eggs from their grain-fed hens. They lived off the land and worshipped and loved without distraction. They focused on each other and on the spirit between them. It was a simpler life, more challenging in some ways but more gratifying in others. Perhaps this is what my grandparents led me to discover—that God is beyond the concrete canyons, beyond the subway tunnels, and outside the cathedrals, in the fresh air of a field of wildflowers at the base of a mountain where the skies are not cloudy all day, the hills are alive with the sound of music, and the streets have no name. The spirits of my ancestors have led me to Montana. The mountain state called to me across the plains, carried by the wind, and in my dreams.

Montana comes from the Spanish word meaning "mountain." It is referred to by locals as God's country. It is my namesake. *Tara,* in Irish, translates as "hill," "highest point," "rocky pinnacle," or "mountain." I know the origin of my first name came from a hill in Ireland. I've seen it written on numerous key chains in Dublin Airport. In fact, this is what my Dublin Airport key chain reads:

> TARA: From the Irish meaning "a hill." A female
> who loves the open air. She is free and cannot be

owned. Her moods are as changeable as stormy skies. She loves faithfully. She is a butterfly to catch.

I never knew the true significance of the historic Tara Hill in County Meath until a friend from Ireland gave me a poster that read, "Save Tara." I also didn't realize I needed saving.

The NRA in Ireland—the National Road Association, not to be confused with the National Rifle Association in America, though both are potentially detrimental to our cultures—was building a motorway through the historic valley where Tara Hill stands, hence the reason for the protest poster. For several years during the construction of the M3, citizens and archaeologists protested the development of the road because it would disturb the landscape of a sacred place. People held sit-ins in front of diggers and machinery to halt the process of the double-tolled four-lane motorway carving its way through the tranquil valley for the sake of progress.

Tara Hill just so happens to be Ireland's ancient capital. It was a pagan sanctuary, a burial ground with remains dating back 3,500 years, and a center where kings were coroneted. It's one of the oldest astronomical observatories in the world. It predates Stonehenge in England and the Egyptian pyramids. Basically, you could say Tara plays a central role in Ireland's cultural identity.

I share in the frustration of the protesters of a motorway that would have disturbed the natural and archaeological landscape of my namesake. I understand because I live near the Boulevard of Death and awaken to the sounds of trains, planes, and automobiles every night as I lie alone in my tiny apartment. I too believe that Tara needed to be saved and in more ways than one.

In the waters of Whitefish, in the bubbling hot tub of a luxurious Montana lodge, I am reawakened. My spirit remembers flying as a brilliant butterfly, feeling nothing but the love of my ancestors, the light in all of us, and the essence of creation. This must be what Toto was talking about when he experienced his NDE.

A female who loves the open air. She is a butterfly to catch. How can I continue to be contained in a city, in a cubicle, in a subway car trapped underground, when I have only just discovered I have wings?

She is free and cannot be owned. She has the capacity to love faithfully. Perhaps it is not a dance partner I am seeking but, rather, the dance itself. Perhaps, as the Lakota Native Americans believe, dance is my religion.

"Tara?" Lauren splashes me as she stands above the hot tub. "You're, like, in a trance. Come on. Your fingers will be pruned, and we have to get ready for dinner."

I didn't realize so much time had passed as I meditated in the water. She hands me a towel as I climb out of my ceremonial bath and realize the distance between me and happiness has grown smaller still.

I don't know what to expect from Bob Grady besides a gentleman in his seventies. I only know he couldn't meet us for dinner until he returned from the nursing home where his wife, Judy, lives and suffers from Alzheimer's. He spends every day with her, from morning to night, feeding her breakfast and dinner, reassuring her with gentle touches and smiles, and waiting for her to fall asleep.

Your worth is determined by your service to others.

If it weren't for the restrictions of visiting hours, he wouldn't leave her side. After fifty-two years of marriage, he still calls her "my Judy."

When I walk down to the lobby of the hotel, I see an older gentleman standing with his back to me, reading a sign.

"Bob?" I say.

He turns around and smiles at me the way my father's father smiled at me in my dream before he walked up to the light. I stop walking midstride, and Bob's face alters.

"What's wrong?" he asks, concerned by my expression.

"It's just that, well, you look like my grandfather Padraic," I say as I extend my hand in disbelief.

"Is that a good thing or a bad thing?" He smiles warmly at me, accepting my handshake.

It is uncanny. It's as if he could be another brother of my granddad from Roscommon, or a son or nephew.

"Oh, it's a good thing. I mean, you look like family." I keep staring at him.

"Do you like your room?"

"Oh yes! We'll take you up after dinner. You must see it. We're so grateful. Really. That was very generous of you."

"Well, it was the least I could do since you were coming here to see me. I was really touched that you'd make the effort."

I wonder if it's possible to like a stranger as thoroughly as I find myself liking this old gent with white hair, wrinkles, and youthful eyes.

As we speak over dinner, I am delighted to learn Bob owned a 1957 Chevy Bel Air. He bought it used in 1959 and put it in his girlfriend's name since he was joining the service. He said it was a way to keep her, as she'd be connected to him through the car, and when he got out of the air force, he married her. Luring a mate with a car seems to run in my family.

After dinner, we bring Bob up to the suite. I don't think he expected it to be as grand as it is. He says he's never stayed in a room like ours. I make him a cup of tea in the kitchen. We sit by the fireplace, and he records a video message for my dad, as Dad is eager to see what he looks like. I am emotional while listening to Bob speak to my father as I sit beside him at the fire. He says he has been looking for our family for a long time, not realizing we were in New York, Roscommon, and London, where my dad's other cousins migrated. He says that due to his situation, he won't be able to visit or go to Ireland again anytime soon. He won't leave his wife in her time of need.

When I walk him to his car, he looks as if he isn't ready to go home. He has just discovered family he never knew existed after searching for many years. He's spent decades looking for us. If it weren't for the internet, we would never have found each other. I promise we'll come back with Dad and the whole family so he can meet everyone. I know I'll return to Montana. I have to return. This is where my spirit was renewed.

In the morning, Lauren and I leave our little oasis and decide to take back roads across the entire state before we return to the impersonal interstate. We think about Bob and his wife, Judy, as we outline the southern perimeter of Glacier National Park. We pass like tumbleweed through the tiny town of Browning, where skinny dogs chase our truck, and Native Americans wearing cowboy hats stand against the walls outside convenience stores, watching us drive. We were warned by some woman in Whitefish not to stop there— not for gas, not for food, not for nothing. I didn't ask why, but I assume she thinks the natives aren't friendly. That's like me telling someone not to stop in some neighborhood in New York. There's good in every hood. We just have to open our eyes to find it and release our fears that keep us from seeing people as people. We are all just people who want to be loved and connect with each other.

We head down toward Great Falls, and somewhere between there and Billings, the road stretches on for miles and miles. We encounter not one building, house, tree, or gas station. I'm concerned I didn't fill the tank back in Whitefish when I had the chance. It is a lonely stretch of land. Even our navigation system ceases to cooperate. OnStar has lost its satellite connection.

"We haven't seen a '57 Chevy in a while." I turn to Lauren, who is dozing beside me in the passenger seat. "I wonder if she's not with us anymore because the road trip is almost over, or we're off her original path."

A few minutes pass. Then, suddenly, Lauren speaks.

"There she is." She points to a tree that appears on the horizon. It is a lonely tree standing independently on a flat plain, and under its branches, shaded by its loving leaves, an abandoned '57 Chevy Bel Air is parked, rusting at her roots.

"Oh my God." I gasp as I look into Lauren's eyes, which are crying and smiling at the same time.

"That just gave me goose bumps." She rubs her forearms.

Tears of gratitude fill my eyes as I tighten my grasp on the steering wheel.

Thank you, Granny Catherine.

29

America—Neil Diamond

North Dakota is closed. Yes, as in the whole state. We have to bypass it because of the great oil rush in Williston, an otherwise sleepy prairie town. Modern-day pioneers are flocking to the state, hitchhiking from as far as California. Every motel, hotel, bed-and-breakfast, and couch is booked across the entire state because they found oil in them there hills—or, rather, under the ground in their fields. All the unemployed citizens in the country have raced to the state to sleep in their cars and brush their teeth out of their trunks in order to earn the almighty dollar in any way that is needed due to the boom. Housing construction is backed up. They don't even have enough teachers or classrooms for all the students arriving with their parents. Thousands of jobs are available, and they can't fill them quickly enough—good-paying jobs too. I could get a job here driving a truck for $80,000.

However, I don't want to live in North Dakota. I just want to drive through it, and unless I sleep in my vehicle, as Granny Catherine did, I will not be able to take her northern route home. This means I'll miss Minneapolis and the Mall of America as well as the Dickeyville Grotto in Wisconsin, which she visited. But it also means we'll be driving through Wall, South Dakota, again.

We call Joseph from the road. The twenty-five-year-old hotel owner is delighted we'll be passing through his small town again, and Lauren is delighted we'll be in the famous drugstore's shops before closing.

"Please let me take you ladies out to lunch," Joseph pleads on the phone. It will be the first time he has ever closed down the main office of the hotel.

With Joseph's hotel temporarily closed and the state of North Dakota temporarily closed to tourists in need of a bed for the evening, I wonder about the American dream. Many people in the country have been laid off. Many are looking for work. My parents never envisioned their daughter struggling. They always assumed I would have more than they had. That is the dream of the immigrant: to create a future for the family. But my future is uncertain once I return this Chevy.

What is the American dream? I've been asking strangers that question all across this land, from shopgirls to gas station attendants, farmers, truckers, teachers, ticket collectors, soccer moms, waiters, business owners, entertainers, artists, and retirees. I haven't been given a unified definition. The consensus is that the dream is defined by the individual. Some say it has to do with success, but that level of success is truly personal. It doesn't have to do with being megarich or owning property. Most people speak of happiness, and that happiness could be brought on by education, financial stability, security, safety, freedom, equality, opportunity, or simply having a better life.

Americans who are born in this country are optimistic. They are born with optimism. They might no longer trust the government or big business, and they might even be protesting at Zuccotti Park down near Wall Street, but surprisingly, they have hope against all odds, even if they don't expect their generation to be better off than their parents. They still have hope.

Immigrants, such as the ones I encounter on the Number Seven subway every day, are the people who keep the American dream alive. They still come to this country, as my mother and my father's parents did, with that belief that if they work hard enough, they can realize the dream they have heard about since they were children growing up in their foreign lands with the idea of America in their heads. Some imagine beaches and gold-covered sidewalks; others simply imagine a place they can sleep in safety without the sound of gunfire or bombs. They sacrifice everything. They give up their lives, families, and friends. They bring their intensity, drive, and passion. They seek a better life, and they refresh our dream each time they come through customs at JFK, swim to shore, or cross a border at night.

This idea of hope, this idea that anything is possible with sweat, hard work, and education, is unique to America. Benjamin Franklin and Martin Luther King Jr. spoke about the American dream. F. Scott Fitzgerald, Arthur Miller, Toni Morrison, and John Steinbeck wrote about it. Barack Obama discusses reclaiming it in *The Audacity of Hope*. This boldness is an American characteristic, one the Asian immigrant acquired on the subway that evening in New York when he asked the woman who was demeaning to him, "Who is in the White House?" The answer was "Hope." We elect these officials because we hope they will bring us to the promised land. We hope they will strive, work hard, sweat, and sacrifice just as we do every single day because they have families and dreams too.

Joseph, the young man with Native American roots, has hope. It's written all over his glowing face. Walking through Wall, South Dakota, with Joseph is like walking with the mayor of a large metropolis. Everyone greets him by name. Everyone winks behind our backs, giving him a thumbs-up for scoring not one but two lovely ladies. They see him driving in our fancy pickup truck at the grocery store. They see him walking around the shops with us at the drugstore. They all have something to say. He is the talk of the town and enjoying the attention.

We order milkshakes and burgers in the famous Wall Drugstore and then make our way to the labyrinth of stores. Lauren heads into a bookshop to buy books about cowgirls and the Wild West. I ask Joseph to escort me into the boot store to help me pick out a pair of cowgirl boots. When I see the prices, I think that perhaps I'll have to pass on the purchase. Most of the boots are more than $500. But then a little old lady informs me that the gold ribbon on certain boots indicates they are on sale. That's when my eyes spy a pair of butter-colored boots with maroon and chartreuse embroidered flowers that look like a Japanese print. They are half price, and when I try them on, Lauren just happens to enter the store.

"You are getting those." It is not a question; it is a command, and as it is coming from my stylist, I have to listen to her.

I am now happy North Dakota was closed. I finally get to purchase my first pair of authentic cowgirl boots. The boots remind me of Luke, the Cody cowboy, and I wonder how he is doing in Georgia or if he has already left for New Zealand on his granny quest.

When we drop Joseph off at his hotel, he asks if he can take a photo with my American flag, the one given to me at the September 11 anniversary dinner. He even sings "See the USA in Your Chevrolet" for my video camera. When we finally say farewell, we hit the road to head east as fast as we can. We have a concert to catch in Chicago in two days. That means at least ten hours of driving each day, including some hours in the dark. I hope we will make it on time.

30

Into the Mystic—Van Morrison

As I speed along Interstate 90, I suddenly notice that the wind on
the plains of South Dakota has picked up. The steering wheel is
becoming a challenge. I look in the rearview mirror and see that the
tarp over the flatbed has unlatched and is flapping up in the wind.
My newly purchased boots are back there, and I don't want to see
them fly off into a cornfield anytime soon.

Lauren and I pull over on the side of the highway, and as we
attempt to get out of the truck, we realize the wind is so fierce it
prevents us from opening our doors. We push with all our might,
climb down from the cab, and run to the back of the truck, where
the tarp snaps up in a gust of wind and flies into the air. We jump
up onto the back of the truck and catch hold of the tarp. It takes
all our might to bring it back into place. But the wind grows even
stronger, lifting the tarp like a balloon in its center, and it forces us
to remain there, holding it in place, as eighteen-wheelers zoom by
us on the busy road.

"It won't go in the latch!" I shout at the top of my lungs over the
sound of the wind.

"Oh my God!" The wind lifts Lauren's shirt as she continues
to grip the edge of the unruly tarp, and a passing eighteen-wheeler
honks at the spectacle of her black bra.

"What are we going to do?" I scream.

"I don't know!" She is just as frustrated as I am.

If we let go, the tarp will snap and possibly smash into the window of the cab, but we can't stand here all day, holding it on the side of the highway under the heat of the South Dakota sun.

"No one is stopping to help!" I keep looking around at all the drivers zooming passed us.

"I have an idea!" Lauren climbs up on top of the flatbed, hoping to use the weight of her body to hold the tarp down long enough for me to latch it into place—but she suddenly disappears when the tarp collapses under her weight.

"Lauren! Are you okay?" I shout over the gale force. When she doesn't reappear, I climb up to find her lying facedown in the truck, unable to get up due to the lumpy luggage and the commanding wind that keeps blowing her back down.

"Hold on!" I shout as I run to the front of the cab. With all my might, I open the side door, and I reach into my bag to find my video camera. This is too funny not to capture on camera.

I've never experienced wind like this in my life. It is even stronger than the wind that woke me the night Granny Nora died in Donegal. The sun is shining over the South Dakota cornfields, there's not a cloud in the sky, and it is eighty-four degrees, but there are no buildings to block the path of the mighty wind on these open plains, and the sheer force of it takes my breath away.

We are eventually able to roll the tarp and tie it back after laughing hysterically as Lauren struggles to get out of the flatbed. We also transfer a number of our lighter items into the cab of the truck for safekeeping, as all our luggage is now exposed to the elements.

The wind makes me wonder about the tornados that destroy many lives in the middle of America. I've always imagined the wind is the breath or spirit of our ancestors. If that is true, then is a tornado all the spirits visiting at once? Are they angry at how we've messed up the world? Is that why Dorothy Gale's house landed on the Wicked Witch of the East?

When meteorologists name a hurricane, do all the Audreys, Bernadettes, and Catherines ride that storm just for name's sake?

Hurricane Tara was one of the deadliest hurricanes off the coast of Mexico in November of 1961. Was I riding that storm before I was born? Did it affect the butterfly migration that year?

Sometimes when the wind blows, I wonder who is kissing my face. Can I only assume it is the spirit of my ancestors, or is it possible that other spirits, those of people I admire but never met, may communicate with me from the beyond? Do they know I think of them, speak of them, read their works, and admire their lives? Or do famous folks only linger with their loved ones and blow kisses on their families' faces through the lips of Mother Nature?

If I could speak with anyone who has passed on, whom would I talk to, and what would I ask him or her? Of course I still want to know what Granny Nora whispered to me the day she died. I also want to ask Jesus why there was money in the Bible in my dream before I saw him in the Garden of Gethsemane. Perhaps Father Peter could explain what the date November 11, 1939, signifies on his tombstone.

But I also have questions for people I've never met. Does Audrey Hepburn know I think of her when I look in my closet each morning and wonder what she would wear? Does Anne Frank know how grateful I am that she kept a diary? I'd also like to ask Saint Bernadette if she forgives me for choosing her name as my holy confirmation name mostly because I adored the Broadway and film actress Bernadette Peters. If I'm considering other questions for saints, I'd like to know why I have to sleep naked on the eve of Saint Andrew's day in order to find a man. That seems absurd, especially since his feast day is November 30, which can be quite cold.

Van Morrison speaks of the wind in my favorite song, "Into the Mystic." He says we were born before it. Granny Catherine had a gypsy soul like the one in the song. Every time I think of her, that song comes on—on the car radio, in Walgreens, or even in my yoga class—and I know it's not a coincidence. I feel certain the Universe speaks to me through music, a language it knows I understand. I clearly hear the foghorn blow as I continue to sail on this spiritual journey into the mystic.

31

Dream a Little Dream of Me—Bing Crosby

I awaken from a vivid dream about a journey as I lie in bed in our hotel in Toledo, Ohio. At one point in the journey, I entered a place that felt like the Garden of Eden. I knew it wasn't the Garden of Gethsemane. I've already been there. I wondered if this new garden was heaven. The most exquisite flamingos, some wearing jewels, stood like royalty in a colony under lush trees draped like weeping willows. The exotic birds waded above the rich dark soil at my feet.

I saw a news report before I fell asleep about the recent death of Steve Jobs and his last words: "Oh wow, oh wow, oh wow." As I was falling asleep, I wondered what he had seen or felt when he passed on to the mysterious unknown, and as I entered the garden in my dream, I too said, "Oh wow," gazing upon the birds. I had the urge to take out my camera but told my dreaming self the scene would best be captured by my mind's eye. So I devoured the colors of the gorgeous birds as I passed through their heavenly realm.

The dream is still fresh in my mind when I wake, and I'm curious to know if it had any significance, because I've never dreamed of these exotic birds. My dream book reveals that it is favorable to see birds of beautiful plumage in dreams, especially bedazzled in bling. Apparently, a wealthy and happy partner is near if a woman has a dream of this nature. He will be my equal because flamingos symbolize balance, as they stand on one leg. When a group of flamingos enter a dream as spirit guides, they are bringing messages from the Divine. *Let go of negativity, focus on the positive, let your inner beauty shine on the outside, connect with your community, and follow your heart, and you will find happiness.*

Ancient Egyptians believed flamingos to be the living representation of the gods. Ancient Peruvians worshipped the birds and often depicted them in their art. Modern Americans place pink plastic flamingo statues in front of their homes to use as lawn ornaments.

Oh wow.

When Lauren is ready, we head down to breakfast in the matching hunter-green T-shirts Monica gave us in the Celtic shop in Butte, Montana. We've spent the past few days driving endlessly and getting on each other's nerves. The road trip has become tiresome. We want our own beds after being on the road for three weeks.

We made it to Chicago on time to exchange the Silverado for the Equinox. As he pried the keys of the Silverado from my hand, Fred Dahling said he had been keeping up with our journey online. I didn't want to part with the truck. I secretly hoped Chevy would let me keep the massive pickup.

We met up with our dancer friend, Fayth, again and took her to the Imelda May rockabilly concert. It was fun, especially when the Dublin-born singer handed me the microphone because she liked the noise I was making in the front row. It's something I learned to do with my tongue to get the attention of musicians onstage. It's called ululation and is often used by Arab women when they are celebrating. Imelda asked the audience if there were any Irish in the house, so I shouted, "Up Donegal!" and she laughed, pointed at me, and repeated Granny Nora's county in her microphone.

Now Lauren and I are tired and grumpy and just want to go home tomorrow, but we have one more task. A fan of my music was able to get me on his local radio station in Toledo that has an Irish music program on Sundays. The program is interested in hearing both my music and my Irish granny road-trip story.

When we slide into our booth in the hotel's dining area for breakfast, our middle-aged waitress approaches the table with an attitude. We can tell we are getting closer to the big, bad city already. People appear to have lost their manners. It started in Chicago. It's as if everyone in a city to the east of the Mississippi River wakes up on the wrong side of the bed.

"What's with the matchy-matchy?" she asks curtly, noticing our green Butte T-shirts.

I am too tired to go into detail. "We're being interviewed on the radio this morning about my cross-country road trip."

Suddenly, the waitress perks up and motions for me to move aside as she pushes her way into my booth. Lauren and I exchange a look.

"Where you ladies from?" She hasn't even brought us coffee yet.

"New York," we answer in unison with less enthusiasm than in previous explanations we've given across the country, now that we are returning to it rather than getting away from it.

"And where did you go?" she asks.

"Seattle," we answer, again in unison.

"So why do they want to interview you?" The waitress won't give up.

"Because I'm on a Chevrolet-sponsored road trip." I wipe the sleep from my eyes.

"Why did Chevrolet sponsor your trip?"

"Because I asked."

"New Yorkers have balls." She shakes her head and then looks at our hands. "Neither of you is married, are you?" She is being bold now.

"Why?" I look at her as I hide my hands under the table.

"No man is gonna marry a gal like you," she says.

"Why not?" Lauren appears offended.

"You're too darn independent. Driving across country on an adventure like that? Nope, men don't marry women like you. You girls sure are something." Then she slides her way out of the booth and begins to walk away before she stops short and turns around. "Did you get coffee?"

"No!" we say, apparently a little too loudly, as we notice other guests turn around from the breakfast buffet.

We didn't realize the radio station was only two blocks from the hotel. If I had known that, I would have left the Equinox with the valet, but we drive down to Water Street and park along the river, where we see a large crowd forming. After I step out of the car, I walk over to a pair of police officers to ask them directions because I can't tell which building the radio station is located in.

"Is it okay to park here, Officer?" I point to the car.

"Oh yeah, it's Sunday, so you're fine," he says, looking back at the crowd.

"What's going on here today?" I ask, wondering what hundreds of people are doing standing by the water's edge on a Sunday.

"They're having a walk for the homeless today." He squints at the crowd.

Your worth is determined by your service to others.

"They took us away from the annual apple-butter festival for this damn thing," the other officer complains.

(Your worth is determined by your service to others.)

I see a white-haired gentleman waving to me from across the street. I assume it is John Connolly, the host of the program *Echoes of Ireland*. He leads us into the building and gets us settled in front of the microphones with our headphones. He doesn't look as if he's had his morning coffee either. As we sit waiting for his cohost, Ted, to arrive, Lauren reminds me to turn off my phone in case it rings during the live program, which is streaming on the internet, so my parents can listen from their home in Queens.

We don't know how long John and Ted are going to ask us questions or which songs they'll play off my two albums. We are more conscious of the time, as we have a long drive ahead of us. We figure we'll have to stop over in Pittsburgh for the night to rest at Lauren's cousin's house and then move on to New York in the morning. We just want to get the trip over with.

The program begins with a bit of banter between John and Ted, who chat about the local weather with no great enthusiasm.

"Eighties in October." Ted speaks with an Irish accent into his microphone. "No heat or need of air-conditioning. At least we can save on the energy bills."

"Indeed, Ted. Any news from Ireland?" John asks his old friend from Galway as he adjusts his eyeglasses.

"No, no. None a'tall. I don't want to talk to them," Ted responds, staring blankly at John.

I wonder how many people listen to this program.

"Well, we have a special guest with us here today. Tara O'Grady traveled the country in her Chevrolet, and we have lots of questions for her. So, Tara, in your own words, tell us how it all came about." John looks over at me.

I explain the whole story from start to finish, from being laid off to making the video for Chevrolet to driving the vehicles across the cornfields while chasing my Waterford granny's spirit the whole way.

"Boy, your mother didn't raise no fool," John says.

His radio program is two hours long. I assume I will tell a bit of my story, he'll play a few songs, and we'll be off on our merry way. But since they have no news to chat about from Ireland and already have discussed the weather in Toledo, the microphone is mine, and I speak for the entire program, with my songs interjected at the appropriate times.

They begin with "Danny Boy."

"Your style of music is much different than mine," John says. "I prefer the traditional Irish, but your renditions are totally different, so I'm told. Let's play one of your tracks now of a song I'm sick of hearing at weddings and funerals."

My voice fills the studio as the two hosts sit back and listen. They don't speak to each other or to us during songs. They just sit and stare at their notes. They didn't listen to my music before I came, so they aren't sure what to expect. The questions fly after the first song ends, and the phone lines light up.

"How did you get this style of singing?"

"Where did you come up with the title *Black Irish*?"

"Who are your influences?"

"Who is your competition?"

"Why did you record in Nashville?"

A sales manager from a local car dealer calls in to the program. He asks me some sort of mechanical question about the Equinox.

"Oh, I don't know things like that, Henry; I just know what color it is," I say into the microphone as Lauren laughs beside me.

"Will we dedicate a song to your Donegal mum, Tara, who's listening in New York?" Ted suggested a song during an advertisement break, as I'm sure he wants to play more traditional songs and not just have my albums dominate the program.

"Yes! Hi, Mom! Ted is going to play this next song for you: 'The Homes of Donegal.'"

The fan who initially got me on the program calls in and asks John if the mayor of Toledo would ever give me the keys to the city.

John covers the microphone. "Now, why the hell would we do something like that? No offense, Tara. Your songs are interesting, and your story is unique, but the keys to the city? She's not a visiting dignitary, but she very well may be a royal pain in the arse." He laughs, looking over at Ted, who quietly gives me the Irish wink.

I don't take offense. I don't need the keys to Toledo. I need the keys to the Equinox. When the program is over, I thank our hosts and then search in my handbag for the keys to the car.

"Lauren, do you have the keys?" I ask, removing numerous items from my purse.

"No, you had them last." She attempts to turn her phone back on. "My battery is dead," she whines.

"Lauren, I don't have the keys. You must have them." I am losing my patience.

"Tara, I told you I don't have them."

The three weeks are almost over. We only have twenty-four more hours to get through, and we'll be back in New York. She is my best gal pal, but it is obvious we need a break from each other.

John can sense a panic attack coming on.

"Now, ladies, I'm sure we'll find your keys. Let's go out to the car. Maybe you dropped them."

I rush down to the street and race to the car. It is locked. I search the ground surrounding the vehicle. Lauren peers through the window to see if the keys are still in the ignition. Nothing.

"What did you do when you got out of the car?" John asks as I look up and down the empty street.

"Um, I spoke with two officers, and there were hundreds of people lining up to do a homeless march." I start walking away from the car, scanning the ground.

Lauren dumps the contents of my handbag onto the sidewalk. When my phone falls out, she turns it on since hers is dead.

"Tara!" she shouts to me as she holds the receiver to her ear. "There's a message from Fred Dahling!"

I run back to the car and grab the phone from her. Fred says he called us from Chicago during the radio program two hours before. Someone found the keys on the street and called the emergency number on the key chain. Fred assumed we were participating in the homeless march.

"John, do you know where the Eire Market is?" I ask.

"Yes."

"Can you drive me there? A man named Patrick has the keys."

Lauren stays by the Equinox as John drives me to a building named after Ireland. *Eire* is the Irish word for *Ireland*. It isn't more than a mile or so from the riverfront. We park and go inside to find the event organizers of the homeless march cleaning up. I approach someone.

"Do you know a man named Patrick? He has my car keys."

"Oh yes, that's him onstage." The woman points to a musician.

The musician saw us enter the building and is already walking over to John with a big smile.

"Tara, this here is one of the best blues musicians in Toledo." John beams at me as he shakes Patrick's hand.

Of course they know each other.

"You saved my life, Patrick!" I shake the musician's hand as he hands me the keys. "Where did you find them?"

"They were on the ground right next to your car. I pressed the button and heard your doors unlock, so I locked them again and brought them here, assuming you were one of the marchers. They've been sitting in the lost and found for the past two hours. You are one lucky gal; we were just about to shut down this place."

I put my hand to my heart as I thank him again, and then we return to John's car.

"Yes, you are one lucky gal." John shakes his head. "What are the chances someone would pick them keys up and keep them safe and not steal the car, which doesn't even belong to you, with all yer laptops and cash and whatnot? How would you have gotten yerself back to New York?"

"Both of my grandfathers' names were Patrick," I say as we drive away from the Eire Market.

"Yes, and Saint Patrick himself is the patron saint of Ireland. So there now."

"What are the chances?" I mutter to myself as I look up at the bright sky above Toledo. Nothing is a coincidence.

32

Get Happy—Judy Garland

There is a photograph of my grandparents visiting my father in the summer of 1962. He was a recruit in the US Army. It was Visit Your GI Family Picnic Day in New Jersey. Dad was twenty-one years old. In the photo, the Bel Air in which he spent the summers of 1957 and 1958 driving across the country with his mother is parked behind him as he and my grandparents sit on the grass with their picnic plates and cooler.

He was just about to be shipped off to Germany, to a US Army base near where Elvis had been stationed, in Wiesbaden, outside Frankfurt. While he was in Germany, Dad's mother purchased her own car for the first time with her own money. It was not a Chevrolet but a 1961 English-manufactured car, the Hillman Minx. She wanted to do another road trip, this time in Ireland, but she would take her own car and not rent one. She put the Hillman on a ship and drove all over Ireland with her daughters while Dad remained at his base outside Frankfurt. They stopped to visit him. It was one of the last great adventures she would take.

When my father returned from his tour of duty in the summer of 1965, his mother was dying of cancer. She was only fifty-eight years old. She passed away in the house just after Christmas, aided by her daughter Cathleen, who had completed nursing school.

My father didn't realize the significance of those two summers he had spent with his mother driving across America in the Bel Air until he returned from Germany, where he had spent precious years away from her, unaware of her developing illness. He didn't know he would lose her so quickly upon his return. There was still so much more to see, do, and say—so many roads not traveled. She would never meet my mother, whom he started dating six months after his mother's death. She would never meet me or my brother. But my father has the memories of that road trip with his mother, and that's why that journey has been so significant in my family's history.

That's why when I see a 1957 Chevy Bel Air, I get emotional. It's more than just a car. It's a member of the family. It's a symbol of my granny Catherine and how she communicated with me while I was on the road trip. It represents the moments in our lives that mean the most to us. To Granny Catherine, it symbolized freedom, adventure, and America. To me, it symbolizes love, spirit, and the idea that life is a precious gift. It's over in the blink of an eye, so you'd better make it the ride of your life.

"I'm moving to Ohio," Lauren announces as we drive over the George Washington Bridge and back into New York City.

"What?" I have been asleep in the passenger seat.

"I've made my decision. I'm moving next week," she says as she turns off the radio.

"Why?" I know I need a break from her, but I don't want to lose my stylist, wingman, copilot, and friend. If there is an art opening or film premiere, a fashion show or live band, she is the one I call. She is my Gal Friday.

"I've had it with New York. I don't want to come back here. This trip changed me—or, rather, confirmed what I've been missing here in this city. I want a family. I want community. I want to belong to a church again."

I am stunned, but I understand what she is saying. This trip has changed both of us. But I have my family in New York, and I don't want to leave them. My parents, my brother and his wife, my nephews, my cousins, the Irish in New York—they are my family, my community.

That's why I continue to put up with living here in the chaotic, congested metropolis where no one looks anyone in the eye. But now I realize there is a pattern to the chaos. I have made connections beyond the subway transfers—and meaningful ones, such as observing the trench-coat couple who were *sole* mates on my morning commute, hearing that violin sing "The Sound of Music," flirting with the Irish guy who asked for my number (and eventually called for one date), and siding with the Asian immigrant who fought for his dignity on the Number Seven train. These are the moments that reveal or awaken, like every time I look at a clock that happens to read 11:11. They are reminders, if we are watching and listening, that the Universe is in sync, communicating its mysteries to those of us seeking translation.

Of all the places I have traveled, I can't imagine settling anywhere else. All New Yorkers have a love-hate relationship with their city. Yes, I'd appreciate more eye contact and interjections of "Bless you" when I sneeze and less traffic and crime. But I thank God my mother and grandparents migrated to this, the greatest city in the world, because where else could I encounter extraordinary moments such as marching down Fifth Avenue with my family on St. Patrick's Day six months after September 11 when a moment of silence was recognized and 250,000 marchers ceased their marching, and bag pipers ceased their piping, and step dancers ceased their dancing, and the millions on the sidelines ceased their cheering so that for one moment all of New York, including the trees in Central Park and the butterflies at the Bronx Zoo, took on a holy stillness, turning around to face downtown where the Towers once stood, until suddenly a wave of sound beginning at Forty-Second Street and rushing like the forceful blow of Old Faithful raced its way up to Eighty-Sixth Street and erupted with such unified emotion, I leapt with the wave of sound as the crest of the roars of millions reached me, and swept me into a harmonious riptide so intense my heart monitor soared.

"So where will you go?" I ask, feeling abandoned already, as if I have just been dumped.

"Cincinnati, where my mother lives. I like the church there too."

We entered each other's lives at the right moment, just after her divorce and just when I was developing as an artist. We've supported each other. But perhaps we have served our purpose, and it is time to move on to other souls.

"Ohio might as well be the Grand Canyon, Louise." I sink into my seat.

"You can visit, Thelma," she tells me.

We finally pull up in front of my parents' house, where my mom; dad; brother, Tom; sister-in-law, Nannette; three nephews, Liam, Connor, and Declan; and aunt Peg are waiting for us. They can't wait to hear our stories from the road, including what we have seen, whom we have met, and what we have learned.

In our matching butterfly-print T-shirts we purchased in a Target outside Chicago, we sit in the backyard and talk over each other while telling stories about lost keys, tornado-like winds, long-lost family, Bel Air sightings in every city or town, milkshakes, lakes, mountains, cornfields, horses and buffalo, blue skies, apple pies and corn on the cob, ghost towns, windmills, and highways that went on for miles with no sign of diesel for sale.

While Lauren is sharing a story about Father Peter's tombstone and how Detective Don placed his foot on the sprinkler to control the Irish mist, I receive an email on my phone. It's from a young Irish American cowboy named Brendan out in Butte, Montana. He is on the committee of the An Ri Ra Irish music festival held each year in August. He writes that he is sorry to have missed me when I was in town, but he heard my music in Monica's Celtic shop and wants to know if I'd like to return to perform at their festival. He also adds that he is single, and I am the type of gal men fight over out west. "It's a battlefield for beautiful women like you, especially ones with talent."

Lauren sees me smiling as I read the email. "What is it?" she asks.

"Looks like I'm going back to Montana." I look up from my phone.

"Not without us!" Dad says.

I put away my phone and pull out a bag with gifts and souvenirs. Most are from Butte. I bought copper earrings for my mom, aunt, and sister-in-law and a few books about the Irish in Montana for my dad. My brother and nephews get some collectibles and other items from the people we met along the way. Declan is so excited about his '57 Chevy Bel Air Matchbox cars that he runs over to my side of the table to thank me. Although he is only eight years old, he has the strength of a gladiator, and as he crushes me with his powerful little arms, he leans into my left ear and whispers something.

"What did you just say?" I ask, pulling him away from me so I can see his face.

He looks at me with the wisdom of an old woman. "I said I love you with all my blood," he repeats. The words sound familiar.

I stare into his eyes, and he smiles back at me. Declan was born nine months after Granny Nora died, nine months after she crushed me with those arms she used for milking cows and picking potatoes. She whispered something to me the day she died, into my left ear, but I couldn't hear it because the blood had rushed to my ears, and I was deafened by my own fear. All these years, I've been wondering what she said to me that morning, and all these years, she's been saying it over and over through my nephew, the grandson who eased my mother's grief when his spirit entered the world.

I love you with all my blood too, Granny. XXX OOO.

33

The Best Is Yet to Come—Tony Bennett

I have a crush on astrophysicist Neil deGrasse Tyson. He makes science sexy. I think it's his enthusiasm. I love watching him get excited about DNA. He says we're all connected. Humans share the same DNA with oak trees and butterflies. He says we are all stardust.

I'd love to have a conversation with him about the music that NASA chose to send into space. They basically threw a message in a bottle out into the Universe in 1977, the year *Star Wars* opened in cinemas across America, with hopes that aliens would eventually receive it and give it a listen on a modern phonograph. I can't even get fans to buy CDs anymore because they don't own CD players. How are aliens going to find a phonograph to play a gold record in deep space?

The *Voyager*'s time capsule contains everything from images to voice recordings of humans speaking different languages on a twelve-inch gold-plated copper record titled *The Sounds of Earth*. It also contains classical compositions by Bach, Beethoven, Stravinsky, and Mozart, plus cultural music from Japan, Peru, and Senegal, and there's even some good old-fashioned rock and roll with Chuck Berry's "Johnny B. Goode." If

I'd been on that committee, I would have included Nat King Cole's version of "Stardust." It's probably my favorite song after "Into the Mystic." But the best tune on that gold record, in my opinion, has to be Louis Armstrong's Hot Seven jazz band performing "Melancholy Blues." Imagine aliens listening to that! I wonder if aliens get the blues. I wonder if they know what it means to feel melancholic, or perhaps they are too evolved as a species to waste precious time on heartache.

The Universe, as most scientists will tell you, is full of mystery. But if we pay attention to the repetitive signs and symbols it puts before us, we can learn to interpret the journey our souls are destined to take. Reflecting on the road trip, I realize now it was the beginning of my spiritual awakening. My daily thoughts informed the Universe I wanted to connect with my spirit and also with the spirits of my grandmothers. By my setting that intention, my life changed, and the Universe guided me, knowing I was open to reading the signs it placed before me on my yellow brick road.

I've always had strong intuition, but I didn't know I could develop this sixth sense we all have but don't often use because we are too distracted by irrelevant details in our daily lives in this modern age. I finally learned how to quiet my mind through meditation. I also started getting acupuncture to reduce stress. The needles act like little antennae, helping me tune in to the frequency of the Universe's main radio station. Now that I'm tuned in to the right channel, I've discovered something extraordinary: I'm clairvoyant!

I had this epiphany one night during a gig. I was on a break, sitting on a stool in Winnie's Jazz Bar at the Refinery Hotel in New York City, telling a guest about my recent trip to Budapest. I was flown to Hungary to present a rare Bible to the House of Houdini. My mother owned the Bible, which was signed in 1893 by the famous Hungarian escape artist Harry Houdini and his father, a rabbi who collected religious texts. Harry signed the Bible using his family name, Ehrich Weiss. Mom acquired the Bible in the 1970s from a neighbor in Queens who used to work for the Weiss family. I sold it on Mom's behalf to a museum based on the famous magician in Budapest. The director of the museum, an escape artist himself, offered to fly me to the city where I'd studied during my university days, and he put me up in a modern hotel.

As I was telling this story in the jazz bar, I finally figured out who put the money in the Bible in the hotel room during my dream in which the wall disappeared to reveal the Garden of Gethsemane. It was a Hungarian escape artist! That was when I realized I was not just intuitive but actually clairvoyant, with the ability to dream of future events. I've been receiving messages in my dreams since I was a child, even with details of past lives of my family members. I dream lucidly of people, places, and things I've never seen in my waking life and learn details about them while I sleep. I dream of everything from the northern lights to the Egyptian queen Nefertiti. I even had a dream recently about a Nirvana cover band living in Belgium. I contacted one of their musicians when I woke up, because he spelled his name in my dream, so I was able to find him online. He most likely assumed I was some crazed fan, but I never knew of his band's existence before I had the dream about them.

I didn't know how to interpret these visions and dreams until now, but I've been writing them down for years. Everything in a dream is symbolic and has a message. It is the way God and the Universe speak to us directly. We simply have to learn how to interpret the language of dreams. The Garden of Gethsemane, as I interpret it, is symbolic of betrayal because it's where Judas betrayed Jesus with a kiss. Harry Houdini's stage act was based on the art of deception, and therefore, his performance was symbolic of betraying the audience. The Bible, the cash, the hotel, and the garden all make sense to me now.

Houdini, an immigrant who migrated to America with his family to chase the American dream, just wanted to seek truth. Yes, his career was based on illusion, but deep down, the man had questions for the Universe. He wanted to learn if there was life after death. He wanted proof that we could communicate with those who have passed on, because after his mother died, he tried to contact her through psychic mediums. He held séances and invited mystics to his home, but all his efforts were futile because he worked in a world of pranksters and didn't have access to honest people with good intentions who didn't want to cheat him. His fame stood in the way of his finding the truth. He then spent the remainder of his life debunking the psychics and mediums he encountered.

Harry didn't know that you don't need to lure greedy strangers to your door with a cash reward of $10,000 to prove there is more to life than meets the eye. Jesus knew that, the Buddha knew that, and even John Lennon knew that. Anyone who can quiet his or her mind and turn inward toward the light inside his or her heart and soul knows that there are many journeys each spirit takes in and out of the 3-D body. This thing we walk around in is just a rental, as my Silverado was, and we exchange our bodies for different journeys, depending on the roads we take.

If Houdini had not used all his negative energy to prove those psychics were false—and they most likely were scammers because of the prize money involved—he could have instead used his positive energy to prove that he himself had the power to connect to a higher consciousness, to God and the Universe, and to his dear mother who had passed on. We don't need a medium or a middleman. We all have intuition. We just have to learn how to develop it, like any skill. We all have a spirit. That is all we need to connect to our loved ones—and faith, as George Michael sang.

My grandparents' spirits have been communicating with me for years in my dreams and in my waking life. They answer the questions in my head through songs I suddenly hear on the radio, or they put before my eyes visions of roosters and butterflies. I even smell chewing tobacco and turf when I am afraid, two distinct aromas that remind me of my Donegal grandfather. When I smell his presence, I know I am safe.

But when we are too distracted by our egos, our intellect, our money or material possessions, and the chaos of daily life, then we don't see the signs, hear the messages, or listen to our own intuition. If we spend our energy in a negative pursuit, as Houdini did, we will most likely attract a negative response. What we think, we become. I suppose Houdini didn't know much about the law of attraction in 1926.

I have never been to a psychic, because like Houdini, I wasn't sure I believed in them. But now that I'm developing my clairvoyance, as any natural ability must be developed, I'm curious to know more about my psychic abilities. Recently, I found myself in a café in New Orleans, and a song entered my head as the waitress poured my coffee. I unconsciously began singing the song to her, and she broke down crying. She revealed that her dad, who used to sing that song to her every day when she was growing up, had just died. This has happened to me more than once, and there is always a soundtrack.

A few months ago, I overheard a woman respond to an intoxicated man at a cocktail party, "I'm not Santa Claus, darling. I don't care if you believe in me or not." Janet, as I learned from a friend, is a psychic. Her confidence, charm, and sass made me like her immediately. I knew I had to go for a reading, especially since, when we were introduced by our mutual friend at the party, Janet immediately informed me that my grandmothers were proud of me.

It is dusk as I ascend the steps of the Italian café on MacDougal Street in New York's Greenwich Village. A saxophone peels from the basement bar next door, which is intentionally called the Bar Next Door. I recognize it as the first place I ever performed a jazz gig many moons ago. The café upstairs is intimate and dark despite its name, La Lanterna.

The psychic medium sits in a cozy corner with tarot cards faceup on her table. She has an elegant style, an air of worldliness about her. The candles illuminate her attractive features and reveal a shy wrinkle or two as she awaits her next customer.

I am that customer.

"Janet!" I approach her tiny table as she rises.

"You are early, my dear." She leans in to kiss me on both cheeks and settles back down as I pull out a chair to sit beside her.

I'm always early, but tonight I am anxious to know what this woman has to say about my life, my future, and my grandmothers, so I am even earlier than usual. I was actually sitting outside in my car for an hour before I entered the café.

She asks me to pull twenty-four cards from the tarot deck and place them facedown in my palm. As I shuffle the pile on the tiny table, I feel as if specific cards call out to me, as if they want to be chosen. It seems to take ages, but when I finally finish collecting the cards, I hand them to her, and she lays them out in a circle.

Her face lights up. "Aha!"

I look at her eyes and then at the cards. "What is it?" I hold my breath as I wait for her to reveal what God and the Universe, as she put it, want to reveal to me.

"You have many admirers, but for some reason, they are not coming forward. Perhaps they fear rejection. You are being loved from a distance." She studies the cards further. "You will marry, perhaps in the next few years, but you haven't met him yet." She looks up at me with caution. "You won't have children of your own. I hope that doesn't upset you."

I look down at the table. "The weird thing is, I've always known that, even as a young girl. I wanted children, but for some reason, I had a premonition that it wasn't my destiny. I've accepted it."

She points to another card. "All four grandparents are deceased?"

"Yes." My heart flutters in anticipation.

She hesitates and sits back. Her face alters as if she is getting a migraine. "There is a woman who wants to speak with you." She pauses to get more information. "She's a singer, a blues singer, and says you would know her by the initial *B*." She looks at me for confirmation.

"*B*? A blues singer? You mean Bessie Smith?" I'm confused. I thought she was going to tell me about my grandmothers.

She shakes her head and looks as if she is listening to someone. "No, no, that's not her."

Then I think about my favorite jazz singer, the woman who said she had a right to sing the blues. "Do you mean Billie Holiday?"

"Yes! That's the one!" Janet pauses and listens.

I'm incredulous. The psychic must have looked up my website when I made the appointment with her. She must know that I love Billie Holiday or that as a jazz vocalist, I must adore her. I mean, come on—who doesn't?

"I want to speak with my grandmothers. There's so much I need to ask them,"

I say, interrupting her, waving my hand in dismissal. I know my grandmothers. The psychic wouldn't know a thing about my grannies. I've waited so long to hear what they have to say to me directly and not through roosters, vintage cars, and songs.

Janet looks at me sternly. "If Billie Holiday wants to speak to you from the beyond, you do not dismiss the woman."

"But why would she want to speak to me?" I'm still reluctant to believe Lady Day herself is trying to communicate with me from the heavens. I'm just some Irish gal from Queens.

Janet clears her throat and then pulls out an empty chair as if to offer it to an invisible guest of honor. "She wants you to know she is honored that you acknowledge her every night when you perform. She wants you to know she's proud that as a woman, you are holding your own in a man's world, know how to manage money, and don't take crap from anyone." Janet makes quotation marks with her fingers at the word *crap*, indicating that Billie did not use that word. "She's amazed you can make your living doing what she did and that you are doing it in a clean way. She wants to thank you. That's all."

I think for a moment, trying to take in those words. I wear a necklace with a photo of Billie when I perform. When I sing her songs, I always mention that she wrote them, and I share her anecdotes I've read over the years. I don't drink or smoke, but I can curse like she did. We are both Aries. Her birthday was April 7, four days before mine. Is it really possible that if we honor the dead, they are aware of our efforts? I only thought we could connect with family and friends, not celebrities or historical figures. That means Audrey Hepburn does know I think of her when I look in my closet and wonder what she would wear. That means Billie Holiday has whispered her songs to me in the wind and landed kisses on my cheek through the lips of Mother Nature.

I look up at Janet. "I wrote a song about Billie called 'Gardenia Girl.' It mentions that she is buried in Saint Raymond's in the Bronx. That cemetery is across the water from my neighborhood in Queens. So basically, I grew up looking over that river, where she has been resting since 1959. I also learned she had Irish roots. Her grandfather was Irish. Her stage name was Billie Holiday, but her real name was Eleanora Fagan."

"Oh my God!" The psychic grabs my forearm. "Tara, I can't believe this. When I was looking at your cards, a woman's voice came into my head, and when she told me her name, I assumed it was my deceased aunt of the same name, so I tried to push her out of my head. But this spirit was persistent. Then it said, 'Tara will know me by the initial *B*. I'm a blues singer.'"

I stare at Janet in expectation.

"Tara, Billie revealed herself with her birth name: Eleanora. God, I love when that happens." She is pleased with her declaration of proof.

Goose bumps form on my arms.

It wasn't until I was introduced to Billie Holiday's voice that I could really sing a song, with my entire being. She sang her heartache. She sang her blues. My ears ached with pleasure in recognition of this shared experience. All I have to do is mention her name, and people respond without words. They throw back their heads, clasp their hands, and gasp, "Oh!"

After the road trip, when I couldn't find a job, I began to sing for my supper full-time because I knew I could carry a tune. I couldn't read music, but neither could Billie. She helped me learn songs, though. Anytime I had to learn a jazz or blues standard, I listened to Billie's version on YouTube. I owe her a great deal. She's my soul sister.

Still having a hard time wrapping my brain around the fact that Billie Holiday just spoke to me from beyond the grave, I try to focus.

"Okay, but what about my grandmothers? I want to confirm what Granny Nora said to me the day she died. She whispered something in my ear. And Granny Catherine—I went on this whole road trip in her honor."

Janet puts her hands up. "One granny at a time." She shuffles the cards and spreads them facedown on the table. "Who do you want to start with?"

"Granny Nora." I sit up straight.

"Pick five, and ask your question," she says.

I pause. "What did Granny Nora say to me that day she died?" I carefully choose five cards and hand them to Janet, who turns them right side up.

I see an image of a heart, a grand lady, a little house, a boy, and a celebration. Janet studies the cards.

"Okay, she wants you to know she was very happy. You brought her great joy when you returned to her cottage every summer with your brother. She looked forward to it every year."

"That's what she whispered in my ear?"

Janet pauses. "No, that's what she wants you to know now." She shuffles the cards and then pulls a single card from the table and smiles. "But when she died, she told you she loves you with all her heart." She holds up the heart card.

I smile, remembering my nephew Declan's words: *I love you with all my blood.*

"What do you want to ask the other granny?" Janet looks at her watch. She has another client after me.

"Um, well, what does she want me to know?"

"Pick five," she says.

We go through the same motions, and the cards are revealed.

Janet laughs. "She's tickled that you are putting her up on this pedestal by telling the road-trip story. She doesn't feel she deserves all the fuss. She's sorry she had nothing to give you, no objects to leave you. She wants you to tell your father she's proud of him and how he raised his family. She's sorry she had to leave him so soon, but she said she's always with him."

"What about Granny Nora? Who is she with?"

"Let's ask the cards."

I choose another five.

"She's with your grandfather, whom she refers to as her soul mate. And she's reconnected with a brother who died young. She's very happy."

Granny Nora had a brother who died in Italy during the Second World War. I sit back and smile to myself, trying to take in all her words, recording them in my brain so I can transcribe the messages to my parents.

Janet shuffles the cards and taps them. "Now, what about romance?"

"What about it?" I ask warily.

"Let's find out more. Who is he, where is he, and when is he coming? Pick five."

As I choose five more cards, Janet begins to laugh.

"What's so funny?"

"Your grandmothers are still offering advice. They are a hoot!" She smiles.

I hold the cards facedown while I finger the edges. "What are they saying?"

"Nora says you should go back to that guy you met on holiday recently in Australia and get married and have a baby with him, but Catherine is saying to stay away from all men, as they are a waste of time and energy, and focus on your work." She lets out a big laugh. "Oh, they are darling!"

I smile to myself. Granny Nora was always such a romantic; even beyond the grave, she claims she is reunited with her soul mate. She'd love to see me settle down with just about anyone. Granny Catherine, on the other hand, the independent 1950s housewife who got her driver's license and left her husband to fend for himself in the kitchen for seven weeks while she took an adventurous road trip, wants me to go it alone and be productive. Such different perspectives from such different women who are both watching over me from above.

"So who is this mystery man?" I say.

"He's coming."

"But when?"

Janet giggles to herself. "Granny Nora wants you to be patient. All your hopes and dreams are going to come true, she tells me." She finally takes the five cards from my hand, faces them upward, and then gasps in delight and reaches out to hug me. "Girlfriend, you hit the jackpot!"

I look at the cards and read them to myself: the Wheel of Fortune, the Star, the Lovers, the Two of Cups, and the Sun.

"So what do they mean?" I look up at Janet.

"Honey, you are going to get it all. Wealth, fame, and a marriage proposal. You will be fulfilling your destiny. Like Granny said, all your hopes and dreams will come true. New opportunities, love—everything! See this?" She holds up the Star card. "You're gonna be a star!"

"I already am. The word *Tara*, in Hindi, means 'star,'" I say.

"Well, that's obvious. There's an aura about you, and you've got some serious guardian angels protecting your every move. I can see them surrounding you—the big ones, like the archangels. But look. This is the most important one." She lifts the Sun card and holds it up for me. "This indicates pure joy." She smiles genuinely. "You are happy by making other people happy with your songs, your stories, and your charisma. You bring joy to other people. And that, my dear, is a true gift."

Now I understand the Divine message that woke me from a dream in the middle of the night and made me get up to write it down.

Your worth is determined by your service to others.

Granny Nora once told me happiness comes from within. "Nothing and no one can make you happy," she said. She spoke of being happy when electricity finally came to her farm. But she was happy before that. There was always a light in her soul, even without electricity. We all share that light, that spark. We are born with it. But somewhere along the road, we forget that luminous exuberance of pure joy, and we become numb.

My journey taught me the Universe is trying to get my attention so I can wake up to my soul's purpose and return to that blissful state I experienced briefly in the butterfly house at the Bronx Zoo. Most of us are sleepwalking through our lives. We are not conscious of the bigger picture, not aware of the wizard behind the curtain, and therefore, we remain distracted, disgruntled, and basically depressed. Happiness is our natural state of being. As Dr. Christine (a.k.a. Glinda the Good Witch) said, everything you want to have, you already do; everywhere you want to go, you're already there; and everything you want to be, you already are. There is no distance between you and happiness, only in your ability to see it.

I now remember my soul's purpose. That's why I felt compelled to share this story with you. Tune in to the songs being played on the Universe's intergalactic radio station. What is it saying to you? Everyone's soul has a different soundtrack. Everyone must embark on his or her own migration to discover the happiness that is waiting to be revealed at his or her core.

I walk down MacDougal Street to my parked Toyota. The sun has set, and the streetlamps cast a stagelike glow on the sidewalk. I start the car and dreamily head toward Houston Street, reflecting on all the things the psychic told me about my grandmothers, Billie Holiday, and my future. When I make a right on Bowery, I turn on the radio. Van Morrison's voice enters my vehicle. It's Granny Catherine's song, "Into the Mystic."

"Of course," I say out loud, and a joyful tear rolls down my cheek.

As I cross the Williamsburg Bridge into Brooklyn on my way home, a calmness I've never felt before comes over me, or maybe I forgot what it felt like—a sense of security, of peace and understanding, as if I know the ending of my story, and it's a good ending, one that is satisfying because it was meant to be and was written in the stars. We are all rock stars, until we are simply stardust.

Bibliography

Dickenson, Emily. "The Chariot." *Poems by Emily Dickinson*. Edited by Mabel Loomis Todd and T. W. Higginson. Boston: Roberts Brothers, 1890.

Frank, Anne. *Anne Frank: The Diary of a Young Girl*. New York: Bantam Books, 1993.

McCourt, Frank. *Teacher Man*. New York: Scribner's, 2005.

Meyer, Dick. *Why We Hate Us: American Discontent in the New Millennium*. New York: Broadway Books, 2009.

Miller, Gustavus Hindman. *10,000 Dreams Interpreted: A Dictionary of Dreams*. New York: Barnes and Noble Books, 1995.

Nepo, Mark. *The Book of Awakening: Having the Life You Want by Being Present to the Life You Have*. San Francisco: Conari Press, 2011.

Ranck, Christine, and Christopher Lee Nutter. *Ignite the Genius Within*. New York: Dutton, 2009.

Sandburg, Carl. "Chicago." *Poetry: A Magazine of Verse* 3, no. 6 (March 1914).

Steinbeck, John. *Travels with Charley: In Search of America*. New York: Viking Press, 1962.

Turner, Erin. *Cowgirls: Stories of Trick Riders, Sharp Shooters, and Untamed Women*. Connecticut: Morris Book Publishing, 2009.

Acknowledgments

Thank you to all the folks who contributed to the creation of this book and the realization of the journey, especially my family who shared their heart monitor stories with me, including my mom and dad, Aunt Peg, and Aunt Cathleen. I am also grateful for my deceased grandparents, who guide me every step of the way with love from above, especially Granny Nora, who shared her words of wisdom with me about the meaning of life and the importance of love and faith. I am indebted to my talented brother, Tom, for making the inspiring video. I treasure my copilot, Lauren, for sharing the journey with me and being my cheerleader as I developed as an artist. Thank you to Chevrolet for sponsoring my road trip, especially the East Hills Chevrolet of Douglaston, Queens, and the DMAX team in Ohio. Your generosity helped me fulfill my dream. I am also grateful to all the folks I met along the yellow brick road who offered beds, tours, meals, free merchandise, hugs, advice, and wisdom. Thank you to my first readers: Maureen O'Brien, B. J. Robbins, Maria Whelan, Colin Broderick, Jeanine Cummins, and Malachy McCourt. Your encouragement and editorial suggestions were greatly appreciated. Thanks also to the professionals at Balboa Press who worked their magic to publish this book.

Made in the USA
Middletown, DE
24 April 2019